CONTENTS

This timely collection draws together a series of reflections based on Scripture that blend Wesleyan theology with application. Written with the benefit of his communal African cultural heritage, Chambo is at one with Wesley in asserting that holiness is always social and personal; but it is never individualistic. This means that God's holiness must be reflected in our lives together: we need to live out our identity in Christ as God's holy people in the mission of God in the broken world that God loves. Of particular importance is his attention to integrity in the public sphere, including the commitment to economic justice and social justice that reflect the heart of God. Chambo addresses the appropriate enculturation of the gospel in specific non-Western contexts but tellingly draws attention to demonic forces such as power and money that subtly enthral Christians in the affluent West. He draws his discussion together by noting that Christian holiness is not a single act, but a lifelong Spirit-empowered way of life. We are called to become who we are in Christ through the Spirit. And we are called to live out this identity together on God's mission.

—Kent Brower
Senior Research Fellow in Biblical Studies
Nazarene Theological College
Manchester, England

This book offers a balanced and winsome perspective on holiness. Drawing insights from his African background and his careful study of biblical texts, Fili Chambo upends our narrow and privatized understandings of the holy life. Throughout the book, he calls us to live out holiness in community and to embody it publicly in our world. This is a picture of holiness that speaks powerfully to people today, one that calls for the transformation of every area of life. I urge you to read this book. But prepare to be challenged!

—Dean Flemming
Author of *Philippians: A Commentary in the Wesleyan Tradition*

Dr. Filimão Chambo has given the church a powerful gift in this book on holiness. Writing as a New Testament scholar, a pastor, and a global leader with a heart for God's people, he reminds us that holiness is not moralism or abstract idealism. For Chambo, holiness is first of all an identity—who we are in Christ because we belong to a holy God. It is both a gift to receive and a calling to embody, made possible by God's enabling grace.

With biblical depth and pastoral wisdom, this book moves holiness beyond private piety into the realities of community, economics, integrity, and public life. It calls us to confess Christ rightly, live in his light, and reflect his character together as the Spirit-formed people of God.

Accessible and deeply practical, this book will challenge and inspire readers to embrace holiness as life shaped by grace and overflowing into faithful witness.

—Gift Mtukwa
Dean and Senior Lecturer
School of Religion and Christian Ministry
Africa Nazarene University

Fili Chambo's theological acumen, along with his experience as a pastor on a global stage, provides him with a rare and expansive look at the ways in which twenty-first-century Christians interpret and edit the call to holiness. We, as fallen humans struggling with the notion of holiness, often impose our own image on God and holiness. Chambo does not let us get away with such self-indulgence. He compellingly reminds us of the unchanging truth of God's character and how it defines our call to holiness. His reflections offer both inspiration and serious warning, intentionally correcting for the evangelical overemphasis on one's personal holiness by relying on John Wesley's foundational tenet that "there is no holiness but social holiness." Truly to be the church requires each believer's personal transformation to be rooted within the communal covenantal relationship of the body of Christ. Chambo does not shy away from identifying sins that trap contemporary Christians around the world; he offers sobering food for thought by identifying the influences of secular culture. He further affirms that the call to holiness involves personal and communal ethical decisions and behaviors, justice, humility, and a commitment to transforming the world today, rather than waiting passively for Christ's return tomorrow. Readers will come away energized, humbled, acutely aware of the allure of secular culture, and emboldened to live in eschatological hope and present-day transformation. This well-balanced and quietly provocative book would be a valuable resource for preaching, small groups, and teen classes and a welcome addition to the collection of anyone seriously seeking genuine life in Christ.

—Mary Lou Shea
Senior Administrative Assistant
Office of General Superintendents
Church of the Nazarene

FOR THE SAKE OF THE WORLD

EMBRACING GOD'S CALL TO HOLY LIVING IN EVERYDAY LIFE

FILI CHAMBO

THE FOUNDRY PUBLISHING®

The Foundry Publishing®
PO Box 419527
Kansas City, MO 64141
thefoundrypublishing.com

ISBN 978-0-8341-4401-9

Cover design: Brandon Hill
Interior design: Sharon Page

Library of Congress Cataloging-in-Publication Data
A complete catalog record for this book is available from the Library of Congress.

PREFACE

The call to holiness is not a relic of a bygone era—it is a living summons for the church today. I began writing this book with a burden and a hope. The burden was for a church that sometimes forgets who it is in the world, tempted by compromise or discouraged by opposition. The hope was that in rediscovering our identity in Christ, we might again reflect the holy love of God with clarity and courage.

This book is a small collection of sermons and talks I have delivered in various settings—district gatherings, university chapels, leadership consultations, and pastoral retreats. These messages were born in real-life ministry, shaped by Scripture, and often refined through the questions, challenges, and testimonies of those seeking to live faithfully in their context. What unites them is a central conviction: holiness is not a peripheral theme, but the heartbeat of the Christian life.

The writing of this book has been shaped by my Wesleyan theological heritage, which insists that grace transforms; by my pastoral ministry across cultures, particularly during my years in Mozambique and across the African continent; and by my current role as a leader in the church, where I have the privilege of witnessing how the call to holiness is being embraced, lived, and tested around the world.

This is not an academic treatise, though it draws from deep theological wells. Nor is it a how-to manual. It is a pastoral and theological invitation to live as a holy people in an unholy world. Holiness is not only possible but necessary, beautiful, and liberating. It is God's gift and our calling.

I am deeply grateful for the many voices who have shaped these reflections—the scholars, pastors, and fellow pilgrims whose wisdom and lives have left their imprint. Above all, I give thanks to the Spirit of God, who calls, convicts, and empowers the people of God to live as a sign of his kingdom. May this book serve that holy purpose.

INTRODUCTION

In every generation, the church must rediscover what it means to be holy. This is not a nostalgic return to moralism or religious performance, but a Spirit-empowered reawakening to our identity in Christ and our vocation in the world. To be holy is to be set apart by God and for God, called not only to avoid sin but also to embody the beauty of God's character in every dimension of life. It is to live as signs of the kingdom amid a broken and bewildered world.

This book emerges from that conviction. It is shaped by a central theological theme: *grace transforms.* The grace that saves is also the grace that sanctifies. The grace that forgives also reorders, restores, and empowers. Holiness is not the result of human striving, but the fruit of divine love received, embraced, and lived.

These pages carry the heart of messages shared over time with fellow pastors, students, and leaders in many corners of the world. Though once spoken in specific moments, they have been prayerfully reworked with the hope that they might speak anew, drawing from Scripture, theology, and real-life ministry experiences.

The Journey of the Book

- **Chapter 1** reflects on 1 Peter 1:13-16, grounding holiness in *identity and transformation.* Peter's call to "be holy, for I am holy" (v. 16) invites believers into a way of life shaped by grace, marked by discipline, and lived in covenantal relationship with the God who calls.

- **Chapter 2**, based on 2 Corinthians 6:14–7:1, explores *separation and discernment*. In a pluralistic world, Paul's exhortation to not be unequally yoked challenges the church to resist spiritual compromise while embodying a distinct identity as God's temple.
- **Chapter 3** moves the focus to Luke 3:10-14 and Acts 4, considering the *economics of the kingdom*. Holiness not only entails private piety but also demands repentance, generosity, and justice in the public and economic spheres of life.
- **Chapter 4** builds on chapter 3's focus by addressing *integrity in public life*, drawing from a theology of salvation that confronts corruption. Holiness is both personal and systemic, calling Christians to reflect God's character in their communities, institutions, and leadership.
- **Chapter 5** centers on the identity of Jesus—the Messiah, the Son of God—and why our understanding of him is the foundation for holy living. Drawing from 1 John, this chapter explores the balance of Jesus's full divinity and full humanity, the dangers of distortion, and the cultural challenges of contextualizing Christ faithfully. It also considers how the Spirit enables the church to confess Jesus rightly, live in his light, and embody his life together.
- **Chapter 6**, based on Philippians 1:3-11, brings the book to a pastoral and communal conclusion. Holiness is not a solitary endeavor, but a *partnership in grace*. Paul's prayer reminds us that love must abound, that our lives must grow in spiritual maturity, and that the church is a Spirit-formed community called to live out the gospel together.

Together, these chapters form a theological and practical vision of holy living: from inner transformation to public witness, from resisting compromise to cultivating community, from personal discipline to societal renewal. Holiness is not a singular act, but a lifelong, Spirit-empowered way of life. It touches every part of who we are and how we live.

You will find throughout this book the voices of Scripture, Wesleyan theology, and contextual reflection—especially drawing from African and global perspectives. These voices offer a hopeful and challenging reminder that holiness is not an abstract ideal. It is the embodied life of Christ in his people.

This book is for anyone who longs to grow deeper in grace, who believes that salvation must change more than the heart, that it must transform how we live, lead, and love. This book is for the church, called to be a holy people in the midst of a hurting world. And it is for those who agree with John Wesley, who strongly rejected inward-focused mysticism that withdrew from active love and service. In a sharp contrast, he wrote, "Solitary religion is not to be found [in the Gospel]. . . . The gospel of Christ knows of no religion, but social; no holiness but social holiness. 'Faith working by love' is the length and breadth and depth and height of Christian perfection."[1]

1. Wesley (1872) 1984c, 321. In the same work, concerning the solitary religion of mystics, Wesley wrote:

> So widely distant is the manner of building up souls in Christ taught by St. Paul, from that taught by the Mystics! Nor do they differ as to the foundation, or the manner of building thereon, more than they do with regard to the superstructure. For the religion these authors would edify us in, is solitary religion. "If thou wilt be perfect," say they, "trouble not thyself about outward works. It is better to work virtues in the will. He hath attain'd the true resignation, who hath estranged himself from all outward works, that God may work inwardly in him, without any turning to outward things. These are the true worshippers, who worship God in spirit and in truth." For contemplation is, with them, the fulfilling of the law, even a contemplation that "consists in a cessation from all works." (321)

Wesley's assertion was not a vague endorsement of communal life, but a sharp theological response to forms of solitary, inward-focused religion that neglected the outward expression of love. "'Holy solitaries,'" he insisted, "is a phrase no more consistent with the gospel than holy adulterers."[2] The gospel of Christ knows no holiness but one that is lived out in community—through "faith working by love," zealously doing good to all, especially to those in the household of faith. Holiness is thus not only personal piety but also Christlike love made visible in relationships, service, and justice.

My prayer is that this book will encourage, challenge, and equip you to embrace this holy calling with joy, humility, and courage. For the God who calls us is faithful. The Spirit who convicts us also empowers us. And the grace that saves us will sustain us to the end.

---

2. Wesley (1872) 1984c, 321.

ONE

"BE HOLY, FOR I AM HOLY": IDENTITY, TRANSFORMATION, AND THE CALL TO HOLINESS IN 1 PETER 1:13-16

Introduction: The Urgency and Relevance of Holiness Today

In every generation, the church must rediscover what it means to live as God's holy people in the world. In an age shaped by secularism, pluralism, and expressive individualism, the call to holiness can sound antiquated or restrictive. But for the apostle Peter, writing to early believers scattered throughout Asia Minor, holiness was not a relic of the past—it was the urgent, present calling of every follower of Christ.

Peter's exhortation in 1 Peter 1:13-16 is rooted in the grace that has already been revealed through Jesus Christ and in the hope of glory yet to come. Holiness, for Peter, is not simply about moral behavior but about identity. It is about being set apart for God, called to live differently because we belong to a different kingdom. "As obedient children," he writes, "do not be conformed to the passions of your former ignorance, but as he who called you is holy, you also be holy in all your conduct" (vv. 14-15, ESV).

The call to holiness is not merely a matter of forgiveness but of transformation. John Wesley envisioned holiness as nothing less than God's gracious work of refashioning us into the likeness we were created to bear—a steady renewal of the divine image that sin had marred.[1] It involves a reordering of the heart, a reorientation of our will and affections, and a life shaped by holy love.

Yet this transformation does not occur in isolation. It is grounded in grace and expressed within the life of a holy community. The early Christians embodied holiness not as an individual pursuit but as a shared way of life. As E. Elizabeth Johnson observes, they did not merely make personal commitments to Jesus but constituted themselves as communities shaped by the in-breaking of God's redemptive realm.[2] Their shared life bore witness to the renewal God had inaugurated through Christ—a renewal marked by porous boundaries, radical compassion, and a commitment to those on the margins. Holiness, then, is not a private endeavor but a public witness, a visible testimony that God is making all things new. It is a communal vocation, rooted in the holy love of God and made manifest in a people conformed to Christ—bearing witness through lives of faithfulness, unity, and the hope of God's coming kingdom.

Throughout this chapter, we will explore 1 Peter 1:13-16 as a rich text that calls the church to reflect God's holy character in a world that often pulls in the opposite direction. We will consider the theological foundations of holiness, the role of the mind and

1. See Wesley 1991a, sec. 3.2; 1991b, sec. 2.1; and 1991c, sec. I.9. In these sermons, Wesley describes salvation as being "'renewed after the image of God,' 'in righteousness and true holiness'" (1991b, sec. 2.5), and links the new birth to the restoration of God's image in humanity.

2. Johnson 2020.

will in the pursuit of transformation, and the implications of holiness for how we live, relate, and witness in the world. Along the way, we will draw from the insights of Scripture, historical theology, and personal ministry experience—including cross-cultural reflections from Africa and the Western world.

The pursuit of holiness is not a withdrawal from the world, but a deeper engagement with it, empowered by grace and marked by love. It is not a badge of superiority but a sign of surrender. Holiness begins with identity, moves through transformation, and results in a life that reveals the beauty of God's character. It is a calling that is both ancient and urgently relevant for today.

Preparing the Mind: A Call to Intentional Transformation (1 Pet. 1:13)

"Therefore prepare your minds for action; discipline yourselves; set all your hope on the grace that Jesus Christ will bring you when he is revealed" (1 Pet. 1:13).

The transition marked by "therefore" in verse 13 signals a movement from theological affirmation to practical exhortation. Peter has already reminded his audience of the living hope they have through the resurrection of Jesus Christ (v. 3), the inheritance kept for them (v. 4), and the joy they experience even amid trials (vv. 6-9). Now, grounded in this hope, the believers are called to live in the light of it. Transformation begins in the mind.

Peter's command to "prepare your minds for action" (v. 13; lit., "gird up the loins of your mind") evokes imagery from the ancient world. In order to move swiftly or engage in strenuous activity, a person would gather up long, loose garments and tie them around the waist. The metaphor suggests alertness, intentionality, and readiness. It implies that the pursuit of holiness is not accidental but cultivated through discipline, attention, and grace-enabled effort.

As Karen Jobes explains, the imperative to prepare the mind "reflects the believer's active participation in holiness. This readiness is made possible through their relationship with Jesus Christ, whose grace enables transformed thinking and holy living."[3] Holiness, then, is not a mere emotional impulse. It involves cognitive clarity and a deliberate reordering of one's thoughts and desires.

This aligns closely with the Wesleyan view of holiness as a transformation of the entire person—heart, mind, will, and affections. John Wesley taught that Christian perfection includes not only purity of intention but also the renewal of the mind according to the mind of Christ. In the words of Paul, we are "transformed by the renewing of the mind" (Rom. 12:2), and Peter echoes this by urging believers to discipline their thinking.

In our contemporary context, this call is strikingly relevant. The modern world often exalts spontaneity and emotional authenticity as the highest values, while dismissing discipline and self-control as restrictive. But Peter's counsel stands in contrast. He invites believers into a life of hopeful vigilance—a mind not shaped by fear or cultural conformity but focused fully on the grace that is to be revealed in Christ.

This grace is both present and future. While we experience God's grace now through salvation, Peter directs our gaze forward—to the ultimate unveiling of Jesus Christ. It is this future hope that sustains present holiness. Abson Prédestin Joseph observes, "Members of the present community are required to display behavior that is characteristic of those who are members of God's family."[4] Their identity is eschatological—it is shaped by who they are becoming in Christ.

3. Jobes 2005, 109-15 (Kindle ed.).

4. Joseph 2012, 84-88.

This call to prepare the mind is not abstract. It touches everyday decisions: how we speak, what we dwell on, how we respond to adversity, how we navigate our digital lives. I once spoke with a university student who believed in Christ but felt fragmented—constantly pulled in different directions by social media, pressure to perform, and internal anxiety. What helped reorient the student's life was a simple but profound practice: each morning, the student opened the day with prayer and the reading of Scripture, consciously focusing the mind on the hope in Christ. It didn't solve every challenge, but it formed in the student a habit of holy attentiveness.

Preparing the mind for action is not about self-effort alone or somehow earning our holiness; it is about surrendering to the Spirit's transforming work and choosing, day by day, to think and live as citizens of God's kingdom. Holiness begins here—in the mind. It is the readiness to live differently because of who we are in Christ and where our hope ultimately lies. God's grace not only forgives but reorients us. It awakens in us the desire to love and obey God in all things. It trains us to think with clarity, act with intention, and live with the joy and discipline of a people set apart.

Resisting Conformity: Holiness as a New Pattern of Life (1 Pet. 1:14)

"Like obedient children, do not be conformed to the desires that you formerly had in ignorance" (1 Pet. 1:14).

Following the call to prepare the mind and fix one's hope on Christ, Peter issues a second imperative: "Do not be conformed to the desires that you formerly had in ignorance." This is a sharp reminder that the call to holiness requires resistance—not only to external pressures but to internal patterns that once ruled the life before Christ.

The imagery of "obedient children" speaks to identity and belonging. To be holy is not primarily about achieving a moral standard but about living in continuity with one's new identity in the family of God. Peter's audience, many of whom were gentile converts, had once been shaped by a worldview that did not acknowledge the holy character of God. Their former desires—driven by self-interest, indulgence, or cultural norms—were rooted in ignorance. But ignorance has given way to revelation. Grace has come, and with it a new way of life.

The verb "conformed" echoes Romans 12:2, where Paul urges believers not to be conformed "to the pattern of this world, but [to] be transformed by the renewing of [the] mind" (NIV). The Greek root (*syschēmatizō*) suggests being shaped or molded—passively taking on the form of something else. In both texts, the warning is clear: unless we are actively being transformed by God's grace, we will inevitably be shaped by the forces around us.

This is particularly relevant in a world where conformity is often rewarded. Cultural expectations around success, image, consumption, and self-expression can subtly (or overtly) shape our behavior and affections. The desires of the old self do not simply disappear; they persist and beckon. Thus, Peter's command is not a call to private moralism, but to a new way of being—a life shaped by a different pattern, rooted in a Christ-centered relationship.

Sanctification involves both putting to death the old self and bringing to life the new self in Christ. This is not a onetime accomplishment, but a continual response to God's initiative. First Peter shares with Romans 6 the vision of becoming who we already are in Christ: those set apart by God's mercy, called to live in faithful obedience through the sanctifying power of the Spirit. Both Peter and Paul make clear, the former desires that once governed our lives no longer define us, but they must be actively renounced.

Paul's language in Romans 6 speaks of a decisive break: those united with Christ in his death are called to "no longer present [their] members to sin" but to "present [themselves] to God as those who have been brought from death to life" (v. 13). Peter echoes this same call in 1 Peter 1:14-16, urging believers not to conform to the desires they formerly had in ignorance but to be holy in all their conduct.

Holiness, then, is not a static condition but a dynamic vocation—a life of resistance to sin and participation in the life of God. Sanctification isn't just a onetime event but also a lifelong process of sanctification (being made righteous). This involves a deliberate turning away from sin and a conscious turning toward God. It's not simply suppressing sinful desires but actively rooting them out as the Holy Spirit transforms our hearts and minds. This requires conscious effort, discipline, and the consistent choice to resist temptation and the pull of our old nature. However, this resistance is not undertaken in our own strength (alone); it is made possible by the grace of God through the atoning work of Jesus Christ.[5] Our efforts are only effective because of the empower-

5. Sanctification demands conscious participation: a daily discipline of resisting the temptations of the old nature. Yet this resistance is not autonomous. It is sustained and empowered by the grace of God made available through the atoning work of Christ. Our new identity in Christ does not erase our vulnerability to sin, but it reorients our lives toward obedience through the Spirit's enabling. As Paul reminds us in Romans 8:11-13, although we still live in "mortal bodies" (v. 11), the Spirit gives life and power to overcome the deeds of the flesh. This aligns with John Barclay's reading of Paul, in which grace is not opposed to obedience but actually generates it. Barclay speaks of the believer as *simul mortuus et vivendi*—simultaneously dead (to sin) and living (to God)—a formulation that captures more aptly than Luther's *simul iustus et peccator* the dynamic tension of the Christian life. As Barclay writes, "Paul's theology of grace is coherent with emphasis on the necessity of human obedience . . . as the product of a divinely created life that is wholly at odds with the normal human condition" (Barclay 2015, 502-3). Holiness, then, is not a static state or the eradi-

ment of God's grace. This growth is not linear or always easy, but it is a real and transformative process.

This passage also underscores the communal dimension of holiness. The "desires" of ignorance are not only personal vices but often socially reinforced norms—ways of thinking and acting that go unchallenged in a fallen world. When the church fails to resist these pressures, it risks losing its distinctive identity. Holiness becomes diluted. The gospel loses its transformative edge.

Here again, Peter's pastoral tone is important. He does not berate his readers for their past. Instead, he calls them "obedient children" (v. 14). This is the language of relationship, not condemnation. It suggests that holiness is not simply a command to be obeyed but a character to be formed—a child learning to reflect the nature of the parent.

As we have noted, Peter's call to holiness urges believers to intentionally break from the ways they previously lived—to no longer allow themselves to conform to or be shaped by the ignorance and cultural norms not grounded in God's truth. They are instead to let themselves be reshaped by the grace and truth of God. This is not a superficial adjustment. It is a deep and often costly transformation. To live as holy people is to live in contradiction to the dominant culture, especially in times and places where faithfulness to Christ invites misunderstanding or hostility. The early Christians Peter addressed were likely facing suspicion, marginalization, and possibly persecution. Their new identity in Christ placed them at odds with family customs, social expectations, and political loyalty. To remain holy in such a context was to remain distinct, even if that meant suffering for doing so.

---

cation of human nature but the Spirit-enabled outworking of a new creation life within the ongoing realities of a fallen world.

In my pastoral conversations across different contexts, I have met many who sincerely desire to live holy lives but feel the weight of the challenges they face in their cultural, familial,

In a church I pastored in Mozambique, I had a candid conversation about holy living with a church member named Matusse.* Matusse was a young professional, and after listening to me, he paused and said, "Pastor Fili, as you know, it is hard to walk in holiness when you are in a culture of honor and shame. Even when you know the way of holiness, how can you say no when your boss expects you to participate in the corruption that is entrenched in the organization? Refusing could cost you your job. And what about honoring your parents or older people in your family? Imagine when they choose to take part in rituals that you know are idolatrous. If you refuse, you dishonor them; if you go to others like your pastor or talk to others in the church to ask for help, you bring shame upon the family."

For Matusse, these were not abstract questions but daily realities. To follow Jesus sometimes meant saying no to expectations that were deeply ingrained in both professional and family life. His countercultural choices often brought discomfort and tension, yet he remained committed to Christ. Over time, he became a respected lay leader in the church, an example of what it means to live as a disciple of Jesus in difficult circumstances.

The call to holiness is never abstract. It touches the everyday decisions of how we speak, how we act, and how we respond when adversity comes.

*Not his real name.

or professional environments. Some wrestle with what it means to follow Christ in a family that worships other gods, knowing that their faith may bring accusations, isolation, or even threats to their safety. Others face moral dilemmas in workplaces where corruption, bribery, and extortion are normalized—and choosing holiness might mean losing their livelihood. Still others struggle with the fear of not belonging, especially when cultural practices, though widely accepted, conflict with the character of the holy God. These are not merely questions of temptation but of identity, loyalty, and courage in the face of real pressure. Yet Peter's call remains: "Be holy yourselves in all your conduct" (1 Pet. 1:15). Holiness, then, is not abstract perfection, but Spirit-empowered witness—faithful living in the midst of hardship, misunderstanding, and even persecution. It is a call to resist compromise, not by our own strength, but by the sustaining grace of the God who has made us his own.

To resist conformity is not to withdraw from the world, but to engage it differently—to live in it with the posture of those who belong to a holy God. The world may say, "Be true to yourself." But Peter says, "Be true to who you are in Christ." Holiness is not repression but restoration. It is not legalism but liberation from the tyranny of misplaced desires. It is not about perfection but about direction: a life moving toward God, shaped by obedience, and sustained by grace.

Be Holy in All You Do: Reflecting God's Nature (1 Pet. 1:15)

"Instead, as he who called you is holy, be holy yourselves in all your conduct" (1 Pet. 1:15).

Having exhorted believers to prepare their minds and resist conformity to their former way of life, Peter now anchors his call to holiness in the very character of God. The instruction is sweeping and comprehensive: "Be holy yourselves in all your conduct." Holiness is not confined to religious activity or private devotion; it encompasses the entirety of life.

The basis for this call is profoundly relational: "as he who called you is holy." Holiness is not merely an ethical standard but the nature of the One who has called us. The God who calls is not arbitrary, impersonal, or indifferent—he is holy, and his holiness is expressed in faithful love, righteousness, justice, and mercy. To be holy, then, is to reflect the nature of the God to whom we belong.

This echoes a deep biblical pattern. Throughout the Old Testament, God's call to Israel to be holy was grounded in his own holiness (Lev. 11:44-45; 19:2). The people of God were to be distinct—not because of superiority—but because they were called to mirror the God who had redeemed them. That calling remains in the New Testament, now extended to the church. Holiness is the visible sign of belonging to the Holy One.

This has significant implications for Christian identity. In Christ, we are not only saved from sin but also called into a new way of being. As Wesleyan theologian Randy Maddox puts it, holiness is best understood as "holy love"—the dynamic expression of God's character formed in the lives of believers. This means that holiness is never just the absence of sin; it is the presence of love, justice, mercy, and truth in how we live.

Peter emphasizes that this holiness must be expressed "in all your conduct" (1 Pet. 1:15). The Greek word *anastrophē*, translated "conduct," refers to one's whole manner of life—behavior, lifestyle, choices, relationships. There is no compartment in which holiness does not belong. This includes how we treat others, how we engage our work, how we use our resources, how we speak, and how we navigate both public and private spaces.

This holistic view of holiness is especially important in a fragmented world. Too often, believers are tempted to divide life into sacred and secular compartments—what we do on Sunday versus how we operate Monday through Saturday. But Peter calls us to an integrated life, where the holiness of God shapes every area of our conduct. Holiness is not a Sunday garment to be worn in worship; it is a daily posture, rooted in grace and lived out in every context.

One of the most powerful witnesses of the gospel today is a life that is wholly and joyfully consecrated to God—a life not perfect, but consistent; not performative, but genuine. When believers embody holiness in their homes, workplaces, neighborhoods, and online spaces, they testify to the reality of a God who is not only holy but also near and transformative. This is not about moral superiority but about relational fidelity. We live holy lives because we have been called by the Holy One. Our lives are meant to reflect that story, not just in doctrine but in deed.

The call to "be holy in all you do" (1 Pet. 1:15, NIV) is both invitation and promise. God's grace does not merely call us to holiness—it enables it. Through the indwelling Spirit, believers are empowered to live lives that reflect God's character. This is the gift and calling of sanctification: not only that we would avoid sin, but that we would increasingly love what God loves and live in a way that makes his character visible in the world.

"Be Holy, for I Am Holy": Imitating the Holy One (1 Pet. 1:16)

"For it is written, 'You shall be holy, for I am holy'" (1 Pet. 1:16).

Peter concludes this sequence of exhortations with a scriptural declaration that echoes through the covenantal history of God's people: "You shall be holy, for I am holy." Quoted from

Leviticus (11:44-45; 19:2; 20:7, 26), this command is both foundational and formative. It affirms that the call to holiness is not a New Testament novelty, but a consistent theme throughout God's redemptive work.

In its original context, the command was given to Israel as a summons to distinctiveness—a life that reflected the covenantal relationship with Yahweh. The people were to be different, not for the sake of difference, but because they belonged to a holy God. Their ethics, worship, relationships, and community life were to bear the marks of God's nature.

Peter invokes this text to emphasize continuity in God's purpose for his people. Just as Israel was called to reflect the holiness of Yahweh, so now the church—Jew and gentile alike—is called to embody the holiness of the One who has redeemed them through Christ. The holiness of God remains the pattern and the promise for his people.

This raises a profound theological insight: holiness is not simply what God commands; it is who God is. And because God is holy, those who are in relationship with him are called to reflect that character. As John Wesley understood, this call is grounded in grace. Wesley wrote, "Gospel holiness is no less than the image of God stamped upon the heart. It is no other than the whole mind which was in Christ Jesus. It consists of all heavenly affections and tempers mingled together in one."[6] For Wesley, holiness is the natural outflow of a life transformed by divine love.

The statement "You shall be holy" (1 Pet. 1:16) is both imperative and indicative. It is a command to be obeyed and a promise to be fulfilled. In other words, holiness is not only what we are called to pursue but also what God, by his Spirit, is forming in us.

6. Wesley 1991b, 340.

This is a hopeful vision. We are not left to strive alone. The God who calls us is also the One who empowers us.

The implications of this truth are far-reaching. In a culture where identity is often self-constructed and where moral relativism can blur ethical lines, the biblical call to imitate God's holiness is countercultural. It is a call to recenter life around the character of God rather than around personal preference or social approval. As Charles Taylor observes in *A Secular Age*, modern identity is frequently formed through self-assertion and internal authenticity, rather than through external moral or theological reference points.[7] But Peter reminds us that our identity is not self-made—it is God-given. We are holy because we belong to the Holy One.

Holiness is not primarily about rule keeping or religious performance but about resemblance. The more we walk with God, the more we begin to reflect his character. As Paul affirms, we are being "conformed to the image of his Son" (Rom. 8:29). But this resemblance is not merely behavioral or symbolic; it is deeply participatory. As 2 Peter 1:4 declares, we are called to become "participants of the divine nature" (Gk., *theias koinōnoi phuseōs*). This identity is not like receiving a new passport—a change in legal status without internal transformation. It is more akin to receiving new blood, a metaphor drawn from Janette Ok's account of identity formation in 1 Peter, signaling a profound, inward renewal that redefines who we are at the very core.[8] The invitation to holiness is, therefore, an invitation to intimacy and transformation—to live in such a way that God's love, justice, and truth are not only expressed through us but have taken root within us.

7. Taylor 2007.

8. Ok 2021.

This perspective liberates holiness from the narrow confines of legalism or perfectionism. Holiness is not a burden—it is a beautiful calling. It is not about earning God's favor but about living out of the favor we have already received in Christ. It is not a list of prohibitions but a life of purpose. It is the Spirit-enabled life that reflects the God who has redeemed us, filled us, and sent us into the world as ambassadors of his holy love.

In practical terms, this means that every Christian—regardless of background, personality, or context—is invited into the lifelong journey of becoming holy. Whether in the pulpit, the classroom, the marketplace, or the home, the call remains: "Be holy, for I am holy" (1 Pet. 1:16). This is both the grounding of our identity and the horizon of our hope.

Conclusion: Holy Living as Public Witness and Spiritual Identity

The call to holiness in 1 Peter 1:13-16 is both timeless and timely. Rooted in the character of God and fulfilled in the grace of Jesus Christ, it invites believers into a way of life that is radically distinct, joyfully surrendered, and deeply transformative. It is not a call to escape the world, but to live within it as those who belong to another kingdom—a kingdom marked by the holy love of God.

Peter's exhortation reminds us that holiness is not a marginal or optional aspect of the Christian life. It is central to who we are. As those who have been called, redeemed, and set apart, we are summoned to reflect the character of the One who called us. This reflection is not limited to religious observance—it touches every sphere of life. Our thoughts, relationships, desires, actions, and ambitions are all to be shaped by the holiness of God.

In a fragmented and morally ambiguous world, the church's distinctiveness is not in its power, wealth, or status, but in its likeness to Christ. The holiness of God reflected in the people of God is a profound witness to the world. It speaks of a love that is pure, a justice that is righteous, a mercy that is deep, and a grace that is transformative. Holiness is not about being removed from the world but about engaging it in a way that reveals the truth, goodness, and beauty of God.

As Wesleyan Christians, we hold that holiness is possible—not by human strength but by divine grace. Sanctification is the work of God in the believer, enabled by the Spirit and nurtured in community. It is both a journey and a destination: a lifelong process of being formed in Christlikeness and a grace-filled goal in which the heart is fully oriented toward the love of God and neighbor. As Paul writes, "May the God of peace himself sanctify you entirely, and may your spirit and soul and body be kept sound and blameless at the coming of our Lord Jesus Christ. The one who calls you is faithful, and he will do this" (1 Thess. 5:23-24). This journey is not a performance, but a participation in God's renewing work. And the destination is not perfectionism, but perfect love—a heart made whole by grace. As we surrender to this work, we are "transformed by the renewing of [our] minds" (Rom. 12:2), so that our lives increasingly reflect the holy love of the One who calls us.

Stanley Grenz reminds us that human identity is ultimately fulfilled in relationship with the Triune God.[9] We are not self-created individuals, but relational beings made in the image of a holy and loving God. As we are drawn into deeper communion with God, our lives begin to reflect his nature. The more we abide in Christ, the more we desire to live in ways that please him. Holiness, therefore, is not external conformity but inward transformation manifesting in outward faithfulness.

9. Grenz 2001.

In this way, holiness becomes a public theology. It bears witness to the reality that God is present, active, and redemptive. In a world that defines identity through brokenness and self-assertion, the church proclaims that identity is received as a gift of grace. We are not our own; we belong to the Holy One who calls us to reflect his image in every aspect of life.

As we conclude this reflection on 1 Peter 1:13-16, the invitation is clear: prepare your minds, resist conformity, reflect God's nature, and live out your holy calling. This is not only about individual piety but also about participating in the redemptive story of God. It is about becoming a community of people who live in such a way that the world catches a glimpse of who God is.

So we return to the heart of the apostolic command: "You shall be holy, for I am holy" (v. 16). This is the calling. This is the promise. This is the witness of the church in every age.

TWO

UNEQUALLY YOKED: HOLINESS, IDENTITY, AND THE CALL TO SEPARATION

2 CORINTHIANS 6:14–7:1

Introduction: Holiness and the Question of Boundaries

In our increasingly pluralistic and interconnected world, the language of separation can feel out of place—even troubling. We celebrate inclusivity, dialogue, and the breaking down of barriers. Rightly so. These are fruits of grace at work in a fractured world. Yet the apostle Paul, writing to the Corinthian church, issues a stark and unyielding command: "Do not be mismatched with unbelievers" (2 Cor. 6:14). Other translations render it, "Do not be unequally yoked" (e.g., NKJV). The message is clear: some alliances are incompatible with the life of holiness.

Why would Paul, who elsewhere urges believers to "live peaceably with all" (Rom. 12:18) and to "become all things to all people" (1 Cor. 9:22), speak in such uncompromising terms here? The answer lies in the nature of holiness as identity and vocation.

Holiness is not merely a behavioral standard; it is a way of being rooted in belonging to God. To be holy means to be set apart by God and for God. This separation is not an end in itself; it is a means by which God's presence is made known through a distinct people.

Paul draws on rich biblical imagery to reinforce his message of covenant faithfulness and holy distinction. His call in 2 Corinthians 6:14 to "not be mismatched with unbelievers" echoes the spirit of Deuteronomy 22:10, where the Israelites are instructed not to yoke an ox and a donkey together. This ancient prohibition symbolized the incompatibility of natures and served as a concrete expression of Israel's calling to maintain purity and distinction within covenant life. By invoking such symbolic boundaries, Paul emphasizes that Christian identity involves more than personal belief—it demands a life aligned with the purposes and character of God.

N. T. Wright, in *Paul and the Faithfulness of God,* argues that Paul reimagines central Jewish symbols—such as temple, covenant, adoption, and cleansing—in the light of the Messiah and the Spirit. These are no longer markers of ethnic distinction but signs of participation in the new creation inaugurated by Jesus Christ. The church, then, is not merely a collection of private believers but a public body, a living temple, called to reflect God's holiness in the midst of the world. Wright writes that Paul's vision is of a renewed people of God, the single family promised to Abraham, shaped around the crucified and risen Messiah, and indwelt by God's Spirit.[1] This renewed people embodies a sacred vocation—marked by moral transformation, relational fidelity, and the indwelling presence of God.

1. N. T. Wright 2013, 729.

Thus, Paul's exhortation is not simply about avoiding moral compromise but about embracing the identity of the church as God's holy temple—a visible sign of new creation. As Wright further explains, Paul's reworking of covenantal symbols serves to demonstrate that the church is now the locus of God's dwelling, bearing witness to the reality that "Jesus is Lord" in a world shaped by rival allegiances.[2] Through holiness, unity, and Spirit-empowered distinctiveness, the church lives out its calling to make God's reign visible in everyday life.

Michael Gorman argues in *Cruciformity: Paul's Narrative Spirituality of the Cross* that Paul's vision of discipleship is not merely about believing in Christ but about being conformed to his self-giving love through participation in his death and resurrection.[3] This cruciform pattern—marked by humility, service, and sacrificial love—is not only personal but profoundly communal, forming the church as a visible embodiment of the gospel. The church, then, is not a private spiritual refuge but a Spirit-filled, covenant community that publicly enacts the justice, peace, and holiness of God. Gorman emphasizes that such participation in Christ transforms the church into the embodiment of the gospel's power and pattern—a cruciform people through whom the Spirit tells the story of God's redeeming love. This vision echoes Paul's own exhortation for the church to be holy and distinct, not in isolation from the world, but as a public witness to the lordship of Jesus Christ.

This message is urgent in Corinth, a city known for its religious pluralism, moral laxity, and complex social dynamics. The Corinthian believers are navigating life in a context where idolatry is not only common but also cultural, political, and rela-

2. N. T. Wright 2013, 723-31.

3. Gorman 2001.

tional. To follow Christ in such a setting requires not only moral conviction but clarity of identity as well. Paul's concern is not that believers withdraw from the world, but that they are not shaped by it in ways that compromise the integrity of their witness and the presence of God among them. James D. G. Dunn underscores this urgency by noting that Paul's vision of holiness flows from the reality of new creation and divine indwelling, not from mere moral striving.[4] Wright affirms that Paul's vision is not monastic withdrawal but mission-shaped identity: the people of God live as witnesses in the world—distinct yet relational, marked by holiness and communal unity.[5]

In many ways, the world of the Corinthians is not unlike our own. Christians today live amid competing loyalties, cultural pressures, and spiritual confusion. The temptation to blend in or compromise is ever present. The challenge of maintaining holy distinction without falling into legalism or isolation is real. Yet Paul's words invite us to reconsider the meaning of holiness—not as exclusion, but as faithfulness; not as moralism, but as missional identity.

Wesleyan theology speaks deeply to this tension. John Wesley understood holiness as both inward transformation and outward witness. For Wesley holiness is "love excluding sin"—a life entirely devoted to God and shaped by love for neighbor.[6] But this love is not sentimental. It is disciplined, discerning, and grounded in the character of God. Holiness, in this view, does not erase boundaries; it redefines them in the light of grace and mission.

4. Dunn 1998.

5. See N. T. Wright 2013, esp. pt. 3.

6. Wesley 1991c, 374.

Unequally Yoked: Identity and Misalignment (2 Cor. 6:14)

"Do not be mismatched with unbelievers. For what partnership is there between righteousness and lawlessness? Or what fellowship is there between light and darkness?" (2 Cor. 6:14, NRSVA).

The Greek term *heterozygountes* (mismatched), used only here in the New Testament, underscores the danger of alignment with unbelievers in ways that impact moral and spiritual direction. Paul is not calling for believers to sever all relationships with nonbelievers; in 1 Corinthians 5:9-10, he acknowledges that such disengagement would require believers to leave the world entirely. Instead, his focus is on binding associations—those that shape one's values, affections, and practices.[7]

In Corinth's pluralistic culture, such associations were frequent and often assumed. Civic festivals, trade guilds, and family expectations drew people into religious and moral environments hostile to the gospel. Believers who yoked themselves to these settings risked confusion, compromise, and divided loyalties. Paul's concern was not withdrawal, but clarity: the people of God must know who they are and live accordingly.

To be yoked with Christ is to be aligned with righteousness and light. To be yoked with unbelief is to be drawn into lawlessness and darkness. The metaphor invites self-examination: What are we joined to? What partnerships, ideologies, or desires influence our directions?

John Wesley addressed this tension by emphasizing that holiness is not about isolation but about the transformation of the entire person—will, affections, and actions—so that one's life re-

7. See Witherington 1995.

flects the character of Christ. Holiness demands not only private piety but also public integrity.[8] Being unequally yoked disrupts this integrity and undermines the sanctifying work of grace.

Today, the temptation to compromise remains. In some contexts, this may involve political allegiances that contradict the gospel, economic partnerships built on exploitation, or cultural practices that blur moral boundaries. Paul's challenge remains vital: the people of God must be shaped more by their identity in Christ than by the pressures of the surrounding culture.

This section of Paul's letter, then, is a call to discernment. What are we binding ourselves to? Where is our ultimate loyalty? In a world full of competing yokes—nationalism, materialism, tribalism, and relativism—Paul urges the church to be yoked to Christ alone.

The Fear Factor: Barriers to Transformation

Why do some Christians continue to live compromised lives, even after turning to Christ? Fear often lies at the heart of the matter. Whether in first-century Corinth or contemporary societies, fear exerts a powerful force—fear of rejection, loss, alienation, or spiritual vulnerability.

For the Corinthian believers, their environment was religiously pluralistic and socially entangled. Many were likely pressured to attend temple feasts, participate in family rituals, or maintain business partnerships steeped in idolatrous practices. Their challenge was not merely theological; it was deeply relational and economic. To walk away from these cultural norms risked exclusion, economic loss, or persecution. As Ben Witherington observes, believers in Corinth faced intense civic and religious pressures, particularly through temple-related commerce

8. See Collins 2007.

and social guilds.[9] Paul's call to "come out" (2 Cor. 6:17) must be read not as a retreat from the world but as a radical reorientation of belonging—to a new covenant community, shaped by loyalty to Christ rather than accommodation to the prevailing culture.

The power of this call lies in its social implications: holiness is not just about private belief but about visible allegiance to a different Lord. This includes moral discernment, yes—but also economic and relational transformation. Corinth was a city where business often demanded compromise, and the pull toward wealth, status, and gratification was strong. These temptations persist. In many African contexts, believers may fear that leaving behind ancestral rituals could invite misfortune or spiritual attack. Some cling to charms or participate in traditional rites "just in case," uncertain whether Christ is sufficient for all of life. In the West, the fears are less overtly spiritual but no less powerful: the desire for success, reputation, sexual freedom, and economic gain often leads to subtle forms of idolatry. As Richard Foster has argued, the demonic strongholds of money, sex, and power are not bound by geography—they are endemic to fallen humanity and intensifying in secular cultures.[10]

In every context, the idols differ, but the fear—and the invitation—remain the same. To follow Christ is to reject cultural captivity and embrace a new story. This is not a retreat into isolation, but participation in a different kingdom. Holiness is not about withdrawal but about faithful presence—a life reordered

9. Witherington 1995.

10. Richard Foster (1985) explores how these three areas—central to human experience—are often distorted by sin and how they can be redeemed through the disciplines of Christian life. He frames them as domains of spiritual warfare and formation, where faithfulness to Christ must be intentionally cultivated.

On a visit to the West African nation of Benin, our guide led us past a Catholic church and a mosque to a voodoo temple, which he called the true center of community life. He explained that many Christians and Muslims still participate in voodoo rituals because, as he put it, "It ties us together." Then he added, "There are things Christ cannot do; only our gods can." His words revealed the grip of fear and the assumption that true belonging requires allegiance to idols.

Yet that same day I heard a very different testimony. A Beninese church leader spoke of Christ's sufficiency and told stories of believers freed from fear and given new identity in Christ. That evening, in worship with church members from Benin and Togo, the congregation sang with passion to Christ alone, proclaiming his sanctifying power over idolatry.

Over a meal, a pioneer church family recounted how allegiance to Christ brought persecution and threats from neighbors practicing witchcraft. Yet every attempt to harm them failed. Their "secret" was simple: full allegiance to Jesus Christ, who proved faithful. In time, some persecutors confessed and came seeking Christ's power.

by grace, rooted in covenant identity, and marked by resistance to the dehumanizing powers of the age.

In many traditional religious systems—including some in African contexts—fear is the dominant motivator. People engage in rituals not out of love or reverence but from a deep anxiety that failing to appease ancestral spirits or local deities will bring curses, illness, or family tragedy.[11] The religion is transactional, and its gods are unpredictable and punitive. But Christian faith offers a radically different vision: God does not demand our loyalty out of terror. In Christ, we do not serve because we fear retaliation; we serve because we have encountered a holy love that "casts out fear" (1 John 4:18). The fear of the Lord is not dread but reverence, awe, and worship. As Wesley emphasized, holiness flows from a heart filled with perfect love, not from hearts shackled by anxiety over divine wrath. This distinction is vital for Christian discipleship in contexts where fear has long shaped the imagination of the sacred.

Wesleyan theology names this fear not merely as a human emotion but as a spiritual condition that is overcome by perfect love. John Wesley expounded on 1 John 4:18, "perfect love casts out fear." As believers grow in the knowledge and love of God, fear loses its hold. Holiness, therefore, is not driven by anxiety but by the assurance of God's abiding presence.[12]

Fear is also a theological issue. When we fear anything more than we fear God, we place that object in the position of authority. Paul's rhetorical questions in 2 Corinthians 6:15 highlight this tension: "What agreement does Christ have with Beliar?" The implication is that any divided allegiance compromises spiritual clarity and weakens the community's witness.

Moreover, fear has the power to distort identity. Those still tethered to fear will find it difficult to embrace the full implications of being God's temple. In contrast, those confident in God's promises—"I will live in them and walk among them" (2 Cor. 6:16)—are freed to live holy lives, not out of compulsion, but out of trust and joy.

---

11. See Mbiti 1990.
12. See Wesley (1872) 1984a, 342.

Thus, Paul's call to separation is not rooted in shame or fear, but in love and hope. The fear of rejection is real, but the promise of belonging to God is greater. The fear of suffering is potent, but the power of Christ's resurrection is stronger. Wesley was clear: the work of sanctification—the process of being made holy—is empowered by grace, not by fear. God works in us "both to will and to do" (Phil. 2:13, NKJV), and our role is to respond with faith and obedience.[13]

The Presence of God—Why Separation Matters (2 Cor. 6:16-18)

Paul deepens his argument by appealing to one of the most profound theological truths in Scripture: the presence of God among his people. "For we are the temple of the living God," he writes (2 Cor. 6:16). This is not merely a metaphor but a declaration of identity and vocation, both individually and collectively. Believers are not only followers of Christ but also his dwelling place, his sanctuary in the world. This declaration draws from the covenantal promises made to Israel and reaffirms that through Christ, God now indwells the community of faith (Lev. 26:12; Ezek. 37:27).

Paul then weaves together a series of Old Testament quotations, forming a theological mosaic: "I will live in them. . . . I will be their God. . . . Come out from them, and be separate. . . . I will be your father" (2 Cor. 6:16-18). These promises are both relational and transformational. They invite the people of God into intimacy and holiness, distinguishing their identity not only by what they avoid but also by whom they are indwelt.

13. Collins 2007, 197.

In the Greco-Roman world, temples were central to civic and religious life. They represented access to the divine and the power of the gods. But Paul radically redefines the temple as the gathered people of God, not a structure made by human hands, but a holy people made new by grace. To be God's temple means to carry his presence wherever we go. As such, holiness becomes not only a requirement but also a response. Separation is not about legalism or fear; it is about reverent devotion to a holy God who dwells among us.[14]

This is where Wesleyan theology offers deep resonance. John Wesley understood the presence of God as purifying, not passive. To be indwelt by the Spirit is to be called into the ongoing process of sanctification—a journey of transformation into the likeness of Christ. The phrase "Wherever the Spirit of God dwells, there is holiness"[15] underscores that God's presence brings not only comfort but change.

The promise "I will be your father" (2 Cor. 6:18) is not just emotional reassurance but a redefinition of belonging. We are not spiritual orphans navigating the world in fear. We are sons and daughters of the Most High, called to reflect the character of our Father. This reorientation of identity shapes how we engage the world. As children of God, we do not mirror the world's values; we embody God's.

In a culture that often blurs moral and spiritual boundaries, Paul's call to "come out . . . and be separate" (v. 17) may seem rigid. But in truth, it is liberating. It frees believers from conforming to systems of idolatry, fear, and compromise. It clarifies our witness and strengthens our community. The church becomes

14. See Witherington 1995.
15. Attributed to John Wesley.

a distinct people, not better than the world, but different for the sake of the world.

This call to holy separation is rooted not in exclusivism but in the very nature of the Triune God. As Tom Noble has emphasized in his 2025 Tyndale Wesley Studies Symposium address, the holiness of God revealed in Israel's worship holds together both divine separation and divine compassion. Holiness involves God's separation from sin, a moral purity that rightly judges what defiles. Yet it also entails God's infinite compassion and covenantal love. These are not opposing attributes but two sides of the same coin. The Day of Atonement, with its rich imagery of sacrifice and mercy, reveals a God who is both transcendent and faithful—utterly distinct from sin, yet deeply committed to his people.[16]

Thus, our identity as God's temple demands both a break from what corrupts and a deeper communion with the holy love of Father, Son, and Spirit. As Noble notes, holiness in Scripture always holds together judgment and steadfast love, separation and presence. We are not called to isolation for its own sake but to be drawn into the sanctifying fellowship of the Triune God, whose presence transforms us and sends us into the world as a holy people.[17]

Kent Brower's work further enriches our understanding of separation in Paul's thought. In *Living as God's Holy People,* Brower emphasizes that Paul's call to be "separate" is not a retreat into spiritual isolation but a covenantal distinction rooted in God's presence. Brower reminds us that the church—now the temple of the living God—is called to embody holiness as a witness, not walling off.[18] In *Holiness in the Gospels,* he argues that holiness in-

16. Noble 2013; 2025a.
17. Noble 2025a.
18. Brower 2009.

volves being kept "safe from the hostility of the world and the power of the evil one, and [being kept] . . . on mission."[19] Brower's synthesis helps us see that spiritual separation is simultaneously a call to reflect divine holiness and to be sent as God's people into the world.[20]

Holiness Perfected—Grace, Cleansing, and the Fear of God (2 Cor. 7:1)

Paul brings his appeal to a powerful and pastoral climax in 2 Corinthians 7:1: "Since we have these promises, beloved, let us cleanse ourselves from every defilement of body and spirit, bringing holiness to completion in the fear of God" (ESV). This verse not only summarizes the theological trajectory of the preceding section but also grounds the ethical call to holiness in God's covenantal grace.

The phrase "since we have these promises" points back to the divine assurances of God's presence, adoption, and indwelling. These are not abstract doctrines—they are the relational

19. Brower 2005, 77.

20. Kent Brower underscores that sanctification is not about removal from the world but about consecration within it. Jesus prays, not for the disciples' escape, but for their protection from the evil one while remaining actively engaged in God's mission. The world, as portrayed in the Fourth Gospel, is the realm of hostility to God—under the influence of the evil one—and simultaneously the object of God's redemptive love (John 3:16). In this context, sanctification means being kept safe from the corrupting forces of the world while being faithfully aligned with God's purposes. The disciples are consecrated "in the truth," which is not merely doctrinal precision but relational fidelity to the One who is the truth—Jesus himself (John 14:6). They are set apart by abiding in Christ and in his word, which guards them against the deceit of the evil one and empowers them for witness. As Brower explains, this sanctifying truth is both revealed in Jesus's person and embodied in his teaching, forming a community that is spiritually protected, missionally sent, and theologically grounded in the redemptive purposes of God (2005, 76-78).

foundations that make holiness both possible and necessary. As James D. G. Dunn notes, holiness in Paul's theology arises from the reality of new creation and divine indwelling, not from mere moral striving.[21]

Paul's use of "cleanse ourselves" is striking. It invites believers into active participation in the sanctifying work of the Spirit. This is not about earning holiness but about cooperating with grace. Holiness is not achieved by retreating from the world but by aligning our hearts and actions with the God who dwells within us. It is a continual process of discerning and removing what corrupts both the body and spirit.

The mention of "body and spirit" reflects the holistic nature of holiness. Paul refuses to compartmentalize. He does not endorse a dualism that treats the body as inherently corrupt and the spirit as purely good. Rather, he affirms that true holiness involves both our embodied lives and our inner dispositions. The Wesleyan tradition echoes this with its emphasis on both inward transformation and outward conduct—what John Wesley called "holiness of heart and life."[22]

To "bring holiness to completion" (Gk., *epitelein hagiōsynēn*) signals an ongoing, progressive work. Wesleyan theology describes this as entire sanctification—a state in which the love of God reigns supreme in the heart, casting out sin and enabling the believer to live in full obedience to Christ. This is not moral perfectionism, but perfect love made possible by God's empowering grace.[23]

And this pursuit, Paul says, must be carried out "in the fear of God." This fear is not servile dread but reverent awe. It reflects

21. Dunn 1998.

22. Wesley (1872) 1984a, 341.

23. Collins 2007, 273.

a profound respect for God's holiness, majesty, and mercy. The fear of God keeps our love from becoming sentimental and our obedience from becoming casual. It is the beginning of wisdom and serves as a constant guard against temptation (cf. Prov. 9:10).

The call to cleanse ourselves, then, is not burdensome—it is a hopeful invitation. It is grounded in the assurance of divine presence and fueled by the Spirit's power. It is God who cleanses, yet he honors our cooperation. As Hebrews 9:14 reminds us, it is Christ's blood that purifies our conscience so that we may serve the living God.

In a culture that prioritizes personal freedom, expressive individualism, and moral ambiguity, Paul's vision of holiness may seem out of step. Yet it is precisely this vision that the church must recover. A people who live in awe of God's presence, who reject both external defilement and internal compromise, and who pursue holiness not out of fear of punishment but out of love for their Savior—these are the people who will bear faithful witness in the world.

Conclusion—Yoked to Christ, Living as a Holy Witness

Paul's exhortation to "not be unequally yoked" (2 Cor. 6:14, NKJV) is not simply a restriction but an invitation to freedom. In Christ, we are called out of darkness not to isolate ourselves from the world but to reflect the character of God within it. Being "set apart" does not mean being "set above." Holiness is a posture not of pride but of purpose: to live in this world as those who reveal the light and love of Christ.

As Jesus prayed in John 17, "They are not of the world, even as I am not of the world. . . . [But] I . . . sent them into the world" (vv. 14, 18, KJV). Holiness means walking in the world with a heart aligned to God's will—living in such a way that our values, relationships, and behaviors witness to the reign of Christ. It is a call to live faithfully, courageously, and distinctively.

In our Wesleyan tradition, this is what we understand as social holiness: not withdrawal from society, but transformation within it. Holiness is not just personal; it is communal and missional. It means living as a people yoked to Christ, submitted to his lordship, and empowered by his Spirit.

To be unequally yoked is to attach ourselves to influences, relationships, or ideologies that draw us away from Christ. Whether it be through cultural compromise, fear, or spiritual confusion, such alignments hinder our witness and erode our joy. Yet Christ offers another yoke—his own. He says, "Take my yoke upon you, and learn from me. . . . For my yoke is easy, and my burden is light" (Matt. 11:29-30).

The good news is that Jesus doesn't merely command—he accompanies. He walks with us. He bears our burdens. And he invites us into a life of freedom, fruitfulness, and faithfulness. Our calling, then, is to live yoked to Christ, resisting what corrupts and embracing what sanctifies.

Let us, therefore, be a holy people—distinct in love, bold in witness, and faithful in all things. Let us walk together, not as those conformed to the world, but as those transformed by grace. Let us be signs of the kingdom—yoked to Christ, filled with the Spirit, and marked by holiness.

THREE THE ECONOMICS OF THE KINGDOM—REPENTANCE, GENEROSITY, AND JUSTICE

Introduction: Economic Holiness in a Materialistic World

In every generation, the people of God have wrestled with a foundational question: "What, then, should we do?" (Luke 3:10). This question, posed to John the Baptist by a diverse crowd, is as urgent now as it was then. We live in a world fractured by economic injustice, distorted by consumerism, and plagued by systemic greed. In such a setting, the call to holy living must include the realm of economics: how we relate to our possessions, how we treat others economically, and how we participate in the structures of wealth and poverty.

Luke 3:10-14 offers a profound and practical vision for economic holiness. This passage is not simply a moral exhortation but a kingdom manifesto, demanding repentance that reshapes every area of life, including economics. John the Baptist does not address doctrinal formulations or ceremonial piety; instead, he speaks directly to how people live, work, and relate to others in tangible economic terms.

In the kingdom of God, economic practices are not separate from the call to holy living. Rather, they are integral to a faithful way of life that reflects the character of a disciple of Jesus. Faithful discipleship encompasses the faithful stewardship of resources, ethical conduct in one's vocation, and acts of generosity that live out our devotion and bear witness to Christ's lordship. As Richard Hays notes, the New Testament writers consistently underscore the economic dimensions of discipleship, urging believers to embody compassion, integrity, and kingdom values in tangible ways. In this light, financial decisions and patterns of giving are not peripheral matters, but vital expressions of allegiance to the reign of God.[1]

This chapter explores how Luke presents economic ethics as central to Christian discipleship. Through the message of John the Baptist and the witness of the early church, we will examine how generosity, integrity, and justice are not peripheral virtues but central expressions of holiness in everyday life. When the Spirit transforms hearts, it transforms hands—how we give, how we labor, how we treat others. The economics of the kingdom are a tangible sign of a grace-transformed life.

The Call to Fruitful Repentance (Luke 3:10-14)

Luke's Gospel introduces John the Baptist not merely as a forerunner of Christ but as a prophetic voice calling people to radical transformation. His message is urgent, disruptive, and unrelentingly practical. When the crowds come to John at the Jordan, convicted by his call to repentance, they ask the most basic and profound question of spiritual transformation: "What,

1. See Hays 1996.

then, should we do?" (3:10). His response is striking—not theological abstraction, but concrete ethical instruction rooted in holy living and economic stewardship.

John does not speak of religious ritual or temple observance. Instead, he addresses how people treat one another, particularly in matters of daily life, resource sharing, and vocational integrity. He calls the crowds to share their clothing and food with those in need. He tells tax collectors to stop exploiting others. He instructs soldiers to stop using their power to extort and to be content with their wages. For John, this is what repentance looks like in action—a visible change in behavior that reflects a renewed heart aligned with God's reign.

In this passage, we see that repentance is far more than a private, internal shift of the heart; it is a public, social, and ethical reorientation of one's entire life. It transforms how economic relationships function and demands a fundamental shift in values. Instead of accumulation, it calls for generosity; in place of exploitation, it requires fairness; and rather than indifference, it compels compassion.

Among the Gospel writers, Luke offers the most vivid portrayal of the socioeconomic implications of the gospel. As Hays suggests, Luke's theology of salvation reflects a deep concern not only for individual transformation but for the renewal of communities and societal structures as well.[2] In Luke's vision, salvation is not confined to the forgiveness of sins—it manifests in ethical practices, resource sharing, and vocational integrity.

This is powerfully illustrated in the crowd's question to John the Baptist in Luke 3:10: "What, then, should we do?" John's reply is direct and practical: "Whoever has two coats must share with anyone who has none, and whoever has food must do likewise"

2. Hays 1996.

(v. 11). True repentance, then, translates into tangible, communal actions. It is not enough to feel sorrow for past wrongs; one must actively engage in redemptive living. The fruits of repentance are made visible in our generosity, our fairness in professional dealings, and our care for the vulnerable. Genuine repentance, in Luke's account, is inherently relational—it restores both persons and the social fabric they inhabit.

It is no surprise, then, that this passage serves as a gateway to Jesus's own kingdom proclamation in Luke 4:18, where he declares that the Spirit of the Lord has anointed him "to bring good news to the poor . . . to proclaim release to the captives . . . to set free those who are oppressed." John prepares the way by calling people to ethical action; Jesus fulfills that call by embodying the justice and mercy of God.

John's message assumes that the people are familiar with God's laws and covenantal expectations. Yet knowledge alone is not enough. Many in the crowd may have known the Torah's commands about caring for the poor, the widow, and the foreigner. But they had not internalized those values in ways that transformed their behavior. The knowledge of the law must be married to the renewing power of the Spirit—a key theme throughout Luke-Acts.

Matthias Wenk rightly observes, regarding Luke-Acts, "The Spirit is not simply the agent of the inspiration of prophetic speech but instrumental in renewing and liberating God's people."[3] This insight highlights a central truth: repentance is not merely an act of self-willed moral improvement; it is a Spirit-empowered reori-

3. Wenk 2000, 151.

entation of one's life toward the justice, compassion, and generosity that characterize the kingdom of God.[4]

John's prophetic call demands that the people reflect the values of the kingdom in their daily choices. Sharing what we have, refusing to exploit others, acting with integrity—these are not secondary expressions of faith, but central signs of transformation. This is the kind of repentance that bears fruit. This is what it looks like to live as citizens of the kingdom of God.

Sharing as an Act of Worship (Luke 3:11 and Acts 2–4)

John the Baptist's response to the crowd begins with a call to share: "Whoever has two coats must share with anyone who has none, and whoever has food must do likewise" (Luke 3:11). In these few words, Luke introduces a radical ethic of generosity that becomes foundational throughout his two-volume work—the Gospel of Luke and the Acts of the Apostles. For Luke, sharing is not simply an act of charity but an act of worship. It is the natural expression of a heart transformed by grace and aligned to God's will.

This ethic of sharing is not limited to a onetime act or seasonal benevolence. It is a lifestyle—a disposition of open hands and open hearts. Importantly, John's instruction is not addressed solely to the wealthy. As several scholars have observed, possessing two tunics or having extra food was relatively normal, even for peasants. The implication is that everyone—regardless of economic status—is called to generosity.

4. As Green (1997, 180) powerfully observes, repentance in Luke's Gospel is never merely an internal feeling or private resolve—it is tangible, relational, and transformative. It takes shape in the public sphere, reordering priorities and reshaping social relationships in the light of God's kingdom.

Luke continues this vision in the book of Acts. The earliest Christian communities, filled with the Holy Spirit, responded to the gospel by forming a radically generous fellowship. In Acts 2:44-45, we read that "all who believed were together and had all things in common; they would sell their possessions and goods and distribute the proceeds to all, as any had need." This was not a legal requirement or communal coercion. It was the overflow of transformed hearts. As Kraybill notes, "The sharing of possessions in Acts does not imply a total loss of them. . . . They become an investment in one's own group."[5]

This sharing is not a rejection of material possessions, but a redefinition of their purpose. In Luke's vision, possessions are not badges of honor or tools for control; they are gifts to be stewarded for the glory of God and the good of others. Luke portrays people as entrusted with God's resources—servants called to extend divine care and generosity.[6] The economy of the kingdom operates on grace, not scarcity; on trust, not hoarding; on interdependence, not self-sufficiency.

For contemporary disciples, this challenges our deeply ingrained assumptions about ownership, entitlement, and individualism. In a world where wealth is often accumulated for personal security and social status, Luke's Gospel invites us to see our resources as sacramental—visible signs of an invisible grace. Giving becomes not only an ethical obligation but a spiritual dis-

5. Kraybill and Sweetland 1983, 238.

6. Kim 1998, 131-67. Luke presents material possessions not as personal assets to be hoarded, but as divine resources entrusted to human stewardship. In his Gospel, wealth is never merely private property—it is a sacred trust. To share generously with those in need is to recognize that all we have belongs first to God and is meant to reflect his care for his children. Acts of generosity, then, are not simply charitable deeds; they are visible signs of faithful stewardship and a deeper acknowledgment that God's blessings are given to be shared, not stockpiled (131-67).

When my wife, Samantha, and I were young pastors at Matola Cidade Church of the Nazarene in the early 2000s, we were overwhelmed by the impact of HIV/AIDS. I was frequently called to conduct funerals, to console families, and to walk with those living with the illness.

As I prayed, the Lord gave me a vision—not only to comfort but to lead the church in responding practically. I invited the congregation to act, beginning with educational events where doctors and psychologists spoke about prevention and care. What followed was beyond my expectations.

A committee formed to guide us, and lay professionals offered their skills and resources with remarkable generosity. Soon groups of church members visited families affected by HIV/AIDS, providing meals, helping with school fees, and offering counseling. In a country without formal hospice services, our volunteers stepped in, sitting with the dying and caring for them with dignity, overcoming the stigma that often surrounded the disease.

The ministry grew into a network that served many churches and communities, mobilizing partnerships and resources. People shared their time, knowledge, and love. Through this witness, many found not only practical help but also the saving grace of Christ. Holiness became visible in a community that shared life so others might live.

cipline—an act of worship, trust, and communion with God and others.[7]

7. See C. Wright 2006.

Moreover, generosity is a visible sign of repentance. It reveals that the power of mammon has been broken and that the Spirit has reordered the priorities of the heart. As James puts it, true religion is "to care for orphans and widows in their distress and to keep oneself unstained by the world" (James 1:27). Holiness is not confined to private piety—it is manifest in compassionate action and just economics.

In this way, sharing becomes far more than a social good. It becomes a doxological act—a public declaration that God is the source of all provision and that we trust him enough to live with open hands. To give is to worship. To share is to declare that we belong to another kingdom, one where grace rules over greed and where love fulfills the law.

Justice in Vocation: Tax Collectors and Soldiers (Luke 3:12-14)

As John the Baptist continues his call for repentance, the message takes a profound turn. Not only are the crowds addressed in general, but also specific vocational groups come forward with a shared concern: "And we, what should we do?" (Luke 3:14; see v. 12). These are not nameless faces; they are tax collectors and soldiers, individuals whose vocations are entangled in systems of greed, coercion, and exploitation. Their question reveals a yearning for integrity in daily life, not just religious ritual.

John's response is both radical and grounded. He does not instruct them to abandon their professions. Instead, he calls them to reform them from within; he calls them to reform their practices. For tax collectors, this means collecting no more than authorized. For soldiers, it means rejecting violence, threats, and dishonesty. In other words, repentance must reach into their public duties and reshape how they handle power, money, and authority. In the Greco-Roman world, tax collectors (Gk., *telōnai*) were notorious for their corruption. Often Jewish collaborators with Roman rule, they were branded as traitors and oppressors, enriching themselves by inflating taxes and preying on the vulnerable. Soldiers (Gk., *strateuomenoi*) were no better, often acting as enforcers for tax officials. They used intimidation, extorted the poor, and manipulated their authority for personal gain. These professions were symbols of systemic injustice—yet John does not dismiss the individuals who hold them. Instead, he invites transformation from within.

This exchange reveals a profound truth: holiness is not confined to personal piety. The ethics of the kingdom reaches into public life. God's call to righteousness transforms how we do our work, how we wield influence, and how we relate to others in professional contexts. Whether in government, business, education, or labor, holy living means embodying the values of justice, honesty, and compassion in every sphere of life.

From a Wesleyan perspective, this vision resonates deeply. John Wesley taught that salvation must lead to social transformation and faithful stewardship in all areas of life—including vocation. He famously declared, "Gain all you can. . . . Save all you can. . . . Give all you can," urging believers to use their resources for the good of others and as an expression of holy living.[8] For Wesley, how one earned, spent, and shared money was not a marginal issue but a deeply spiritual concern. For him, holiness was never abstract; it had to be lived out in the real world, particularly through just and faithful vocation.

Luke's message still confronts us today. In a world marked by exploitation, unjust wages, corporate greed, and systemic inequality, the call to justice in vocation remains urgent. The baptized and repentant are summoned to embody a different way—a

8. Wesley 1991d, 356.

kingdom way—in how they manage businesses, serve clients, lead institutions, and treat workers. This is not simply about ethical behavior; it is about bearing witness to God's reign in the ordinary rhythms of work and service.

Whether one is a teacher or a technician, a farmer or a CEO, a soldier or a sanitation worker, the invitation is the same: bear fruit in keeping with repentance. Holiness must inhabit the workplace as fully as the worship space. When our vocations are shaped by the justice and mercy of God, the world begins to glimpse what it looks like to live under the lordship of Christ.

Redefining Poverty, Wealth, and Social Status

One of Luke's most significant contributions to New Testament theology is his consistent effort to redefine societal values—especially those surrounding poverty, wealth, and honor. From Mary's Magnificat (Luke 1:46-55) to the Beatitudes (6:20-26), from parables like the rich fool and the rich man and Lazarus (12:13-21; 16:19-31) to the radical generosity of the Acts community, Luke portrays a kingdom where God upends conventional power structures and rewrites the meaning of status.

At the heart of this redefinition is a vision of human worth and social responsibility grounded, not in material wealth or heritage, but in God's mercy and justice. In the ancient Mediterranean world, wealth and honor were often seen as divine favor and societal approval. The poor, by contrast, were marginalized, voiceless, and often seen as morally inferior. Luke directly confronts these assumptions.

In Luke's Gospel, the "poor" are not defined merely by economic destitution, and the "rich" are not condemned simply for their abundance. Rather, the concern is relational and theological. As Mel Shoemaker observes, individuals such as Naaman (see 2 Kings 5)—despite being socially powerful—are depicted as "poor" in the Lukan sense because they are spiritually needy and dependent on divine mercy.[9] Poverty, in this framework, becomes a metaphor for openness to God, for acknowledging one's vulnerability and dependence.

Conversely, wealth becomes dangerous, not because of its existence, but because of its tendency to insulate, to foster pride, and to entrench social and spiritual separation. In Luke 16, the sin of the rich man is not merely that he is wealthy but that he is blind to the suffering of Lazarus who lies at his gate. In Luke 12, the error of the rich fool lies not simply in storing grain but in his misplaced trust in possessions rather than in God. Yet these texts may also critique not only trust in wealth but also the failure to share it. The impulse to store rather than to share reflects a failure of stewardship—a heart turned inward that forgets abundance is not meant for personal security alone but entrusted by God for generosity and the well-being of the wider community.

This reframing carries profound implications for the church. In the kingdom of God, the scales are not balanced according to market value or social pedigree. Instead, the lowly are exalted and the self-secure are scattered. Mary's song, often seen as the overture to Luke's theological drama, boldly declares this reversal: "He has brought down the powerful from their thrones and lifted up the lowly" (1:52).

Luke not only challenges social stratification but also offers a blueprint for a new kind of community. The Acts community models this vision—not by erasing individual identity—but by rejecting systems that assign worth based on wealth, heritage, or status. When "no one claimed private ownership of any possessions, but everything they owned was held in common" (Acts 4:32), it was not merely an act of redistribution. It signaled a re-

9. M. Shoemaker 1992, 181-205.

pudiation of the world's categories of power and privilege. They were embodying a new identity in Christ, where mutual care replaced competition and honor was redefined by sacrificial love rather than accumulation.

Crucially, Luke does not condemn wealth in absolute terms, but he does expose its dangers. Wealth, in his narrative, is often entangled with exploitation and spiritual blindness. It can easily take on an idolatrous role that hinders genuine discipleship (Luke 18:24-25). Yet the wealthy are not beyond redemption. Figures like Zacchaeus demonstrate that the rich can be transformed and included in the people of God through repentance and restoration. Likewise, Luke does not romanticize poverty. The poor are lifted up, not because of any inherent virtue in poverty itself, but because they are often more ready to receive the kingdom with humility and trust.

In this new community, everyone is called to live under the lordship of Christ—a call that demands humility, compassion, and responsibility. The kingdom does not erase differences but reorders them according to divine values, challenging both the hoarding of wealth and the idealization of suffering. It calls all—rich and poor alike—into a new economy of grace, where generosity, justice, and mutual belonging prevail.

This vision has particular relevance today. In a globalized economy marked by staggering wealth disparities, where privilege is often inherited and poverty perpetuated by structural injustice, the church must recover Luke's radical message. Holiness is not about escaping the world but about transforming it. It means confronting systems that diminish human dignity and advocating for those left behind.

It also means teaching believers to see themselves and others differently. The wealthy must see their abundance not as entitlement but as responsibility. The poor must be seen not as objects of pity but as bearers of God's image, recipients of his promises, and essential members of the body of Christ. Status is defined no longer by possessions or popularity or power but by the grace of God and our participation in his redemptive work.

Luke's Gospel thus becomes a theological and ethical compass. It invites us to live in a community where wealth is shared, honor is given to the humble, and every person is valued as God's beloved. This is the society that holiness builds—a Spirit-filled community where economic practices reflect divine priorities and where social relationships are healed by the justice of the gospel.

A Spirit-Empowered New Community (Acts 4:32-35)

The early Christian community in Acts offers one of the most powerful illustrations of what happens when the transforming grace of God reshapes not only individual lives but also corporate relationships. Acts 4:32-35 presents a compelling vision: "Now the whole group of those who believed were of one heart and soul, and no one claimed private ownership of any possessions, but everything they owned was held in common. . . . There was not a needy person among them" (vv. 32, 34).

Luke is intentional in highlighting this moment. It is not a brief aside but a theological statement. The generosity of the believers, their unity of heart, and their shared resources are a continuation of what began at Pentecost—the outpouring of the Holy Spirit that ignited a new creation. This new community is the fruit of the Spirit's work. It is a living answer to the question asked in Luke 3: "What, then, should we do?" (v. 10).

The language of "one heart and soul" (Acts 4:32) echoes the Hebrew understanding of covenant community. This is more than emotional unity; it is covenantal solidarity. The believers saw themselves as one people, one body in Christ. This oneness did not dissolve individuality, but it bound them together in mutual love and responsibility. The presence of the Spirit reoriented their affections and priorities. The economy of grace replaced the economy of self.

One of the most radical expressions of this new community was the attitude toward possessions. Luke does not portray the early believers as coerced or legislated into communal ownership. Rather, they willingly and joyfully relinquished personal claims in order to meet the needs of others. This generosity was not transactional—it was transformational. It revealed a deep conviction that everything belonged to God and was to be used for his purposes. Yet Luke also includes a sobering narrative in Acts 5:1-11—the story of Ananias and Sapphira, who pretended to participate in this communal generosity while secretly withholding part of their gift. Their deception was not in the amount given, but in their attempt to appear generous while violating the Spirit-led integrity of the community. This contrast underscores the point: true stewardship is not merely about financial giving but about living with transparency, trust, and a wholehearted commitment to God's mission. As Beverly Roberts Gaventa notes, the story functions as a warning against hypocrisy within a Spirit-formed community.[10] Likewise, Luke Timothy Johnson emphasizes that the narrative highlights the necessity of communal integrity as a vital expression of faithfulness in the early church.[11]

Importantly, Luke distinguishes this Spirit-led community from other known models of communal life in antiquity. The Qumran community, for instance, had strict legal structures for property sharing. Greco-Roman households operated on patron-

10. See Gaventa 2003.

11. See L. Johnson 1992.

age and obligation.[12] But the early church modeled something altogether new: voluntary, Spirit-driven sharing that emerged from love and grace, not law or social pressure.

This distinction is vital. The generosity in Acts was not rooted in ideology but in identity. Their sharing flowed from who they were in Christ—a new people, called to reflect God's kingdom on earth. As such, their economics were spiritual. Their stewardship was sacramental. Their unity was a testimony to the resurrected Christ.

Moreover, Acts 4 frames this economic sharing as an integral part of the apostolic witness: "With great power the apostles gave their testimony to the resurrection of the Lord Jesus, and great grace was upon them all" (v. 33). The connection is clear: the proclamation of Christ's resurrection was accompanied by the visible embodiment of resurrection life—a community where injustice was being undone and the needs of the poor were met in practical, redemptive ways.

This image of the church as a Spirit-empowered economic fellowship challenges contemporary ecclesiology. Too often, the church has adopted the world's categories of success, hierarchy, and accumulation. But Luke's portrait reminds us that the Spirit leads the church not into privilege but into service, not into self-preservation but into sacrificial love. The Spirit unites us not only in doctrine but also in economic solidarity.

For today's church, the vision of Acts 4 is not a historical relic—it is a prophetic invitation. It calls us to reimagine our communities as places of radical generosity, mutual care, and shared responsibility. It challenges us to examine how our budgets, programs, and lifestyles reflect—or betray—the kingdom of God.

12. See Kraybill and Sweetland 1983.

When the Spirit fills the church, the result is more than emotional enthusiasm or miraculous signs. It is a renewed people who live differently—who give freely, love deeply, and dismantle the barriers of class, race, and wealth. As MiJa Wi insightfully argues, the Holy Spirit in Acts is both a boundary crosser and a boundary marker, empowering believers to move beyond inherited divisions while shaping a new identity grounded in God's mission.[13] In this sense, the Spirit's work is inherently social and communal, forming a holy people whose economic life and relational practices reveal the character of God.

In this way, Acts 4 is not only descriptive but prescriptive. It shows us what is possible when grace takes hold. It invites us to pray, not only for revival but also for the courage to live as a Spirit-formed people—together, generous, and transformed. A community where no one is in need because everyone lives openhandedly before God and one another is not a fantasy. It is the fruit of Pentecost. It is the church, empowered by the Spirit and rooted in the cross.

Kingdom Ethics: Holiness, Justice, and Economic Discipleship

Holiness in the kingdom of God is not a private pursuit detached from the rhythms and realities of everyday life. It is not merely about maintaining personal piety or avoiding individual sin. Rather, in Luke's theological vision and throughout the early church's witness, holiness is deeply ethical, communal, and economic. It transforms how we live, how we work, how we relate to others, and how we manage what has been entrusted to us.

13. Wi 2019b.

The ethical implications of repentance are made clear in Luke 3:10-14, where John the Baptist calls people to concrete actions: share what you have, act justly in your vocation, and be content rather than exploitative. These are not optional moral enhancements; they are fruits worthy of repentance. In this way, Luke reminds us that the call to holy living cannot be severed from justice, integrity, and generosity.

Throughout Luke-Acts, we see a repeated refrain: discipleship involves transformation in all areas of life, including the economic. The tax collector Zacchaeus exemplifies this when he voluntarily offers to give half of his possessions to the poor and to repay fourfold anyone he has defrauded. Jesus affirms this not as extraordinary but as expected evidence of salvation: "Today salvation has come to this house" (Luke 19:9).

This vision challenges modern discipleship models that reduce holiness to spiritual disciplines alone. Of course, prayer, Scripture reading, and worship are essential. But as the prophets and Jesus repeatedly insist, if those practices are not accompanied by justice, mercy, and compassion, they become empty rituals. Holiness is not confined to the altar—it must overflow into the street.

George Eldon Ladd's interpretation of kingdom ethics is instructive here. He notes that Jesus's teaching does not abolish the law but radicalizes it, moving it from external regulation to inner transformation. "The primary emphasis," he writes, "is on the inner character that underlies outward conduct."[14] Murder becomes a matter of anger. Adultery begins with the eye. Generosity is not measured in amount, but in intent. This shift makes ethics a matter of the heart—a heart shaped by grace, filled with the Spirit.

14. Ladd 1993, 127.

In this sense, economic discipleship becomes a vital dimension of holy living. It asks, How do we treat others with our financial power? Do we use our wealth to elevate ourselves or to bless the community? Are our business dealings marked by fairness and compassion? Do our lifestyles reflect a commitment to simplicity, generosity, and trust in God's provision?

Too often, Christians have separated their financial lives from their spiritual lives. The church may speak about tithing or giving, but broader conversations about debt, consumerism, global inequality, or ethical investment are less frequent. Yet Luke and Acts suggest that these are not peripheral issues—they are central to discipleship. When the Spirit comes, it not only prompts prayer but also liberates resources, inspires generosity, and cultivates new economic practices rooted in kingdom values.

This has practical implications for pastors and congregations today. Economic discipleship must be taught, modeled, and nurtured. Churches must become places where people learn not only how to pray but how to spend, how to give, how to steward, and how to live justly. Preaching and teaching must address greed, injustice, and fear, not with guilt, but with hope and grace.

The kingdom of God offers a new way of being in the world—a way in which wealth is shared, needs are met, vocations are dignified, and the poor are honored. Holiness is not an escape from the world but a commitment to it—a holy presence that transforms unjust systems and heals broken relationships. Justice is not a political sideline; it is a gospel imperative.

Economic discipleship, then, is not merely about charitable giving. It is about a life patterned after Jesus, who though rich became poor for our sake (2 Cor. 8:9) and who calls us to follow him in sacrificial love. It is about embodying kingdom ethics in the office, the market, the budget meeting, and the grocery store.

It is about living, not from fear or greed, but from the abundance of God's grace.

In a world shaped by scarcity and competition, the church is called to be an alternative society—a holy people whose economic life bears witness to a different King and a different kingdom. This is not idealism; it is discipleship. It is what it means to take up our cross, deny ourselves, and follow Jesus—daily, practically, and sacrificially.

Conclusion: Transformed by Grace, Living with Open Hands

Luke 3:10-14 opens with a deeply human, timeless question: "What, then, should we do?" This question echoes in every heart touched by grace. It emerges when repentance is real and when the Spirit convicts us not just of sin but of the need for transformation. John the Baptist's response, as we have seen, is profoundly practical: share what you have, act justly in your work, be content with what you earn. These instructions serve as more than moral advice—they represent a new way of living under the reign of God.

What Luke presents throughout his Gospel and the book of Acts is not a disconnected set of teachings but a coherent vision of holy living in a world shaped by injustice, inequality, and spiritual blindness. It is a vision in which grace transforms not only the soul but the whole person—relationships, ethics, economics, and community life. The church, filled with the Spirit and shaped by repentance, becomes the living embodiment of this vision.

Holiness is not about retreating from the world but entering into it with new eyes, new values, and new purpose. It means no longer living for self but for God and others. It means renouncing the idolatry of possessions and embracing the joy of generosity. It means treating wealth, not as a badge of identity or a fortress of security, but as a sacred trust to be stewarded for God's glory and our neighbor's good.

To live with open hands is to live with the humility of Christ. It is to imitate the One who "though he was rich, yet for your sakes . . . became poor, so that by his poverty you might become rich" (2 Cor. 8:9). It is to acknowledge that all we have is a gift and that all we are belongs to God. It is to resist the culture of accumulation and to live with gratitude, simplicity, and compassion.

John Wesley's famous exhortation to "gain all you can, . . . save all you can, . . . give all you can"[15] was not a license for ambition but a call to stewardship. Wesley's theology was rooted in grace that transforms—grace that moves outward in love, grace that reshapes how we relate to money, status, and power. He warned repeatedly of the dangers of riches, not because they were inherently evil, but because they so often seduce the heart away from God.

In today's global context, where economic inequality has become one of the defining issues of our time, Luke's message remains prophetic. Holiness is not indifferent to poverty, nor is it detached from justice. When God's people are transformed by grace, they become agents of transformation in the world. Their generosity bears witness to the abundance of God. Their justice reflects the character of the King. Their community life becomes a sign of the kingdom that is already breaking in.

This is what it means to be the church. It is not just a gathering of believers but a Spirit-filled people who share life, who share resources, who share burdens, and who shine as a light in a dark world. It is a people who live the answer to the question, "What, then, should we do?"

---

15. Wesley 1991d, 356.

We are called to live generously, not because we are wealthy by the world's standards, but because we have received mercy. We are called to work for justice, not to earn righteousness, but because we serve the Righteous One. We are called to embody the economics of the kingdom—to live with open hands because our hearts are rooted in grace.

The early church held no political power, commanded no armies, and wielded no cultural influence. Yet they turned the world upside down—not through violence or status, but through holy living, selfless giving, and Spirit-empowered witness. Some, like Barnabas, used their possessions to bless the community. Others, like Ananias and Sapphira, serve as warnings against hypocrisy and self-serving faith. The point is not that no one had wealth, but that those who followed Jesus were called to hold it lightly and share it freely. They fed the hungry, welcomed the stranger, cared for the sick, and gave sacrificially. In doing so, they made visible the love of the invisible God.

May the same be said of us. May we be known not merely for our theology but for our generosity, not merely for our doctrine but for our compassion. May our lives reflect the holiness of God in how we spend, how we give, and how we love. For when the church lives with open hands, it reveals the open heart of God to a world longing for hope.

Let us be transformed by grace. Let us embrace holy living in everyday life. And let us show the world what it means to belong to the kingdom of God.

FOUR
SALVATION AND THE SCOURGE OF CORRUPTION—A CALL TO HOLINESS IN PUBLIC LIFE

Introduction: A Crisis of Character and Systems

Corruption is a cancer that eats away at the moral fabric of societies across the globe. It undermines institutions, deepens poverty, sows distrust, and multiplies injustice. Though it manifests in public offices, political systems, and economic practices, its roots are deeper and more spiritual than they appear on the surface. Corruption is not merely a political or economic issue—it is fundamentally a spiritual crisis, a manifestation of human sinfulness, and a rebellion against God's righteous order.

"Corruption falls squarely in the moral realm because it is symptomatic of the original sin that marks the heart of every person."[1] It is born from the depravity of the human heart and cannot be adequately addressed through policy reform alone.

1. Schenone and Gregg 2003, back cover.

Greed and moral compromise are spiritual issues requiring spiritual remedies. The church, therefore, must go beyond issuing moral commentary; it must engage prophetically by proclaiming and embodying the gospel that transforms hearts, renews minds, and restores relationships.

Any meaningful response to corruption must be grounded in the biblical doctrine of salvation, which encompasses not only the forgiveness of individual sins but also the transforming power of God to make people holy, restore broken communities, and heal the nations. Without this foundational understanding, efforts to fight corruption become moralistic, short-lived, or co-opted by the very systems they seek to reform.

In this chapter, we will explore how a robust theology of salvation speaks directly to the scourge of corruption. We will examine biblical texts, theological reflections, and pastoral implications for a church that must not only proclaim salvation but also embody it as a witness in a broken world. The Wesleyan vision of holiness—deeply concerned with personal and social transformation—offers a compelling framework for this challenge. The task before us is not simply to analyze corruption but to recover and champion a vision of salvation that changes hearts and societies alike.

Understanding the Nature of Corruption

At its core, corruption is the misuse of entrusted power for personal gain. But beneath the surface of transactional dishonesty lies a deeper theological crisis. Corruption is a rebellion against the holy character of God, who is just, faithful, and true. It distorts justice, denies dignity to the vulnerable, and perpetuates cycles of exploitation and inequality. It is a spiritual distortion that flows from the heart of fallen humanity.

African theologians have rightly observed that corruption is not just a legal or political issue but a moral and theological crisis that reflects a failure to live under the lordship of Christ. It includes practices such as bribery, extortion, and the abuse of power, all of which undermine the justice and holiness of God. As Kwabena Asamoah-Gyadu notes, corruption reveals a spiritual disorder and the erosion of accountability before divine authority.[2] Some African thinkers and public theologians—such as Tinyiko Maluleke, in his public commentary and journalistic writings—have underscored the importance of distinguishing between perpetrators and victims in discussions about corruption. Those who are extorted under duress should not be seen as morally culpable in the same way as those who abuse their positions for personal gain. The prophetic task of the church, therefore, is not only to denounce corrupt systems but to embody a new kind of society marked by honesty, justice, and integrity. As Emmanuel Katongole argues, the church must form communities that live as public witnesses to God's alternative kingdom—offering hope, modeling transformation, and resisting the normalization of evil.[3] In doing so, the church proclaims that salvation is not limited to personal piety but includes the renewal of society through the grace and truth of Christ.

Scripture is unambiguous about God's abhorrence of corruption. The prophets denounce dishonest gain, bribery, and the perversion of justice with piercing clarity. Isaiah cries out, "Your princes are rebels and companions of thieves. Everyone loves a bribe and runs after gifts. They do not defend the orphan, and the widow's cause does not come before them" (Isa. 1:23). Micah condemns leaders who judge "for a bribe," priests who "teach for

2. Asamoah-Gyadu 2013.
3. Katongole 2011, 76-78.

a price," and prophets who "give oracles for money" (Mic. 3:11). These texts reveal that corruption is not a new phenomenon. It is as old as sin itself.

In biblical thought, the root of corruption is idolatry,[4] placing anything above God and seeking fulfillment in false sources of power and security. Whether it is wealth, status, tribal loyalty, or unchecked ambition, these idols capture the human heart and lead to actions that violate God's commands and harm others. From a Wesleyan perspective, sin is not only the wrong things we do but the distorted affections that drive us—what Wesley called "inbred sin." Therefore, corruption is not merely a matter of behavior but of a disordered heart and nature. The answer to corruption, then, is not superficial reform but deep transformation—the kind that salvation in Christ alone can bring.

This perspective becomes even more urgent in the African context. The moral crisis of corruption in Africa cannot be separated from the failure to live out the values historically embedded in African communities. African societies have long affirmed the ethical principles of Ubuntu,[5] a moral philosophy rooted in humanness, shared dignity, and mutual respect. As Desmond Tutu[6]

4. Salvation is incomplete without outward transformation. True holiness embraces both inward purity and a holy passion for justice—responding to the wronged and resisting evil. Systemic corruption, in this light, is not merely a political or cultural failure but a spiritual rebellion—a disorder of the heart marked by misplaced affections and ethical apathy. It is the tragic substitution of God's justice with the idols of self-interest, power, and indifference.

5. Ubuntu is a comprehensive ancient African worldview based on the values of intense humanness, caring, sharing, respect, and compassion, ensuring a qualitative communal way of life.

6. Desmond Tutu (1931–2021) was a South African Anglican archbishop, theologian, and Nobel Peace Prize laureate. As chair of South Africa's Truth and Reconciliation Commission, he became a global moral voice advocating for restorative justice rooted in Christian theology and the African ethic of Ubuntu. His views on forgiveness and reconciliation carry weight not only because

often explained, Ubuntu teaches that "my humanity is caught up, is inextricably bound up, in yours. I am human because I belong."[7]

Yet, despite the high moral ideals of Ubuntu, the persistence of corruption reveals a deeper spiritual deficiency. While Ubuntu deemphasizes individualism and prioritizes communal integrity, some in the modern African societies have increasingly embraced individualistic, materialistic, and self-serving patterns of life. In this context, one would not think it necessary to have a new set of anti-corruption policies to regulate African affairs if the moral values depicted here were embraced. The tragedy is that the philosophical values of Ubuntu and the theological vision of holiness have both been sidelined—replaced by systems that reward greed and punish integrity.

Even more troubling is that many who engage in corruption still identify as Christians. This points to the danger of a generic or nominal Christianity, one that embraces religious identity without a deep commitment to the ethical demands of the gospel. While there are many faithful and spirit-formed disciples of Jesus across Africa, the rapid growth of independent Christian churches (including prosperity-gospel movements) has not always been matched by intentional discipleship that forms integrity in public and personal life.

The church must therefore recover its prophetic identity. It must teach that corruption is not merely a violation of civil law but a rejection of God's holiness and a distortion of his image in humanity. As N. T. Wright argues, "The call of the gospel is the call to share in the life of the new creation—where God's justice, holiness, and truth are meant to reshape the lives of God's

of his theological insights but also due to his leadership in guiding a nation through the wounds of apartheid toward healing and hope.

7. Tutu 1999.

people here and now."[8] The church must call people not merely to ethical improvement but to repentance—a radical reorientation of the heart, empowered by grace. As Thomas Noble affirms, salvation restores God's image in believers, forming a people whose character reflects Christ's compassion, generosity, and love. This transformation is participatory and grace driven, shaping a community that resists evil and embodies God's holiness in every sphere of life.[9] As Paul wrote to Titus, "The grace of God has appeared, bringing salvation to all, training us to renounce impiety and worldly passions and in the present age to live lives that are self-controlled, upright, and godly" (Titus 2:11-12).

Salvation as Personal and Public Transformation

Salvation in Scripture is comprehensive. It is not limited to justification—the forgiveness of sins—but includes sanctification, the ongoing work of the Spirit to make people holy, and the restoration of God's image in them. Holiness, as taught in the Wesleyan tradition, is not about withdrawal from the world but about righteousness, love, and justice lived out in every sphere of life.

This truth is powerfully illustrated in the story of Zacchaeus. When this tax collector encountered Jesus, he didn't merely pray a private prayer of confession. He immediately pledged to give half of his possessions to the poor and to repay those he had defrauded fourfold (Luke 19:8). His salvation had economic and social implications. Jesus responded, "Today salvation has come to this house" (v. 9). Here, salvation is not only a moment of spiritual forgiveness but also a visible transformation that disrupts patterns of injustice and exploitation.

8. N. T. Wright 2010, 69.
9. See Noble 2013, esp. p. 112 (Kindle ed.).

This aligns with Luke's broader emphasis on discipleship that touches every area of life. Luke reconstructs the soteriological narrative to show that discipleship should affect all spheres of life, rather than a narrow private realm. The discourse between John the Baptist and those seeking baptism (3:10-14) underscores this holistic view. John's call to repentance addressed concrete socioeconomic behaviors—sharing with the poor, refraining from extortion, and practicing contentment. This is not moralism but transformation rooted in grace.

Theo-ethically, salvation cannot be severed from integrity. As already demonstrated elsewhere in this book, John Wesley consistently emphasized that authentic Christianity is expressed through love for God and neighbor, active compassion, and public witness. He warned against any version of faith that remains inward and isolated, urging believers to embody holiness through works of mercy, justice, and social engagement. For Wesley, to be truly saved was to be fully committed to a life that reflects the character of Christ in both personal conduct and societal responsibility.

The New Testament affirms that those who are in Christ are new creations (2 Cor. 5:17). This newness touches every dimension of life—personal, relational, ethical, and public. As Robert Wall notes, the Wesleyan reading of salvation "presses for a more collaborative notion of salvation . . . God's grace forgives, heals, transforms, and ultimately sanctifies the believer to respond in active and ever perfecting love toward God and neighbor."[10] A transformed life will naturally bear the fruit of righteousness and justice. This is the challenge facing the church: to move from nominal belief to embodied holiness.

10. Wall 2000, 102-3.

There is a danger that some may already view corruption as an acceptable way of life, getting involved in petty corruption activities because of need and/or greed. This tragic disconnect between faith and practice reveals the failure of a narrow gospel that neglects public discipleship. The result is a Christianity that coexists with corruption rather than confronting it.

The church must resist the temptation to reduce salvation to a private escape from judgment. The gospel is not transactional; it is transformational. When the grace of God captures a life, it produces integrity, humility, generosity, and a passion for justice. These virtues stand in stark contrast to the greed, deceit, and abuse of power that characterize corruption.

True conversion does not produce passive consumers of grace but active participants in God's mission of reconciliation and justice. Sanctifying grace is the power by which believers are renewed in love and empowered to live holy lives. Such lives challenge corruption not only by rejecting it personally but by actively seeking the renewal of broken systems.

The Church as a Prophetic and Holy People

The church is not called merely to comment on corruption; it is called to be a holy counter-community, a visible sign of the kingdom of God in a world ravaged by sin and injustice. As the body of Christ, the church is meant to embody God's holiness and justice in every domain of life. When the church lives faithfully, it becomes both a prophetic witness against corruption and a transformative agent for integrity and righteousness.

In the Old Testament, Israel was set apart to reflect God's character among the nations: "You shall be holy, for I the Lord your God am holy" (Lev. 19:2). This holiness was not abstract or merely ceremonial. It involved ethical living: honesty in business, protection for the poor, care for the foreigner, and justice in judgment. Similarly, the church—as the people of the new covenant—is called to reflect the holy nature of God by how it lives, loves, and leads.

However, the credibility of the church's prophetic voice is tied to its own moral integrity. A church that tolerates or participates in corrupt practices forfeits its capacity to call the world to repentance. As Jesus warned, "If salt has lost its taste, how can its saltiness be restored? It is no longer good for anything" (Matt. 5:13). Holiness, therefore, is not optional; it is the very ground of the church's mission.

The church must be Scripture shaped and Spirit formed. It is expected to have an ethical influence on the life of the people, not merely through its preaching but by its visible lifestyle. In Luke-Acts, "the Spirit is not simply the agent of prophetic speech but instrumental in renewing and liberating God's people."[11] The church's prophetic presence must flow from this Spirit-empowered holiness.

This prophetic holiness is not confined to sermons or institutional statements. It is demonstrated through modeling integrity in church finances, leadership, and decision-making; empowering disciples to resist corruption in their professions; and confronting injustice not only in the world but within its own structures.

The church is not perfect—but it is called to be purified. It is a living body, not a pillar of stone—organic, dynamic, and always in process. As a community being sanctified by grace, it must continually return to repentance, receive forgiveness, and be restored and transformed by the Spirit. Holiness is not a static achievement but a lifelong journey of becoming more like Christ. This journey unfolds, not in isolation or retreat from the world,

---

11. Wenk 2000, 151.

but within the concrete realities of human life—amid hardship and temptation; these are not abstract dangers but real forces the church contends with daily.

Yet holiness is not simply about resistance but about grace-empowered faithfulness in the trenches of life. It is about learning to walk in the Spirit when confronted by injustice, to choose integrity when compromise is more convenient, and to love faithfully in a world that often rewards selfishness. The church is called to reflect God's character in the very places where that character is most lacking.

Even in this struggle, the church remains committed to truth and shaped by the Spirit into a holy people. Our primary task is still to "prepare the way of the Lord" (Luke 3:4; see vv. 4-6). That preparation includes preaching salvation with both pastoral care and prophetic courage, calling individuals and communities into the lifelong journey of Christlike discipleship—a journey that is sustained not by human effort alone but by the transforming power of grace.

John Wesley envisioned the church as a visible society of holy people, deeply engaged in acts of mercy, justice, and reform. The early Methodist movement bore witness to this through prison reform, labor advocacy, and social holiness. Wesley warned that if the movement ever lost its prophetic edge, it would become "a dead sect, having the form of religion without the power."[12]

This warning is particularly poignant today. The church must reclaim its prophetic voice, not in self-righteousness, but

12. Wesley (1872) 1984d, 258. In 1786, Wesley lamented, "I am not afraid that the people called Methodists should ever cease to exist either in Europe or America. But I am afraid, lest they should only exist as a dead sect, having the form of religion without the power. And this undoubtedly will be the case, unless they hold fast both the doctrine, spirit, and discipline with which they first set out" (258).

in Spirit-filled boldness. It must stand as an alternative to compromised business, politics, and ecclesial structures. While the philosophy of Ubuntu continues to affirm values such as interdependence, hospitality, and mutual respect, it is only when these values are transformed and empowered by the Spirit that they can become truly redemptive.

Salvation and Institutional Integrity

Salvation is not limited to individual transformation—it extends to the transformation of institutions. While institutions cannot be "saved" in the same way as people, they can be reformed, redeemed, and reordered through the influence of those who have been transformed by God's grace. The church's mission, therefore, must include equipping believers to engage structures of power with holy integrity.

Institutions—whether governmental, educational, commercial, or ecclesial—shape the lives of people in profound ways. When marked by corruption, favoritism, and greed, they become tools of oppression rather than instruments of service. But when infused with the values of God's kingdom, they can promote justice, equity, and human flourishing.

Scripture offers compelling examples of godly individuals who brought about institutional reform. Joseph's integrity in Pharaoh's court, Daniel's faithfulness in Babylon, and Nehemiah's leadership in Jerusalem all demonstrate how personal holiness can influence public systems. In each case, their deep commitment to God enabled them to serve with courage, wisdom, and effectiveness in corrupt environments.

As already stated, there should be no sphere of life that is not under the authority of Jesus Christ. This means believers must see their vocations not merely as employment but as missional placements. A teacher who refuses bribes, a judge who

During my years as a pastor, I often heard stories of believers who faced the daily pressure of corruption in their workplaces. Some, sadly, gave in to the system. But others stood firm, even when it cost them opportunities. One such example came from a Christian professional who worked in the national health sector.

One time, a supplier attempted to bribe her with an enticing offer. Instead of ignoring him, she asked if he had children. When he replied yes, she pressed further: "Do you want your children to follow the example you set?" The man admitted he did. She then explained, "I was raised in a family with principles, and I must live by them. Please respect that. The process for our contracts is clear, just follow it, and we will guide you if you need help." Days later, her director called to thank her for her professionalism.

Her integrity did not go unnoticed. Though she faced criticism for being "too rigid," her refusal to compromise earned respect from some who were older and more experienced. She eventually rose to leadership, not through shortcuts, but through faithfulness.

Her story is a living witness that salvation is not only about private spirituality but about holiness in public life, resisting corruption and trusting God with the results.

resists political pressure, a business owner who pays fair wages, and a church leader who insists on transparency—each is living out salvation in public witness. These acts are not ancillary to discipleship; they are expressions of the kingdom.

This becomes a witness that grace transforms not only the heart but also outward relationships and responsibilities. As Ray

Dunning notes, salvation involves a "full-orbed" holiness that affects the entire person—mind, will, relationships, and ethical engagement in the world.[13]

Institutional corruption thrives when people abandon these virtues. In some parts of Africa, systemic corruption is one of the most significant barriers to development and justice. Public officials delay services unless bribes are paid, and national resources are diverted for personal enrichment; financial mismanagement undermines credibility. The tools and means that are put in place to address corruption are costing the world a lot of money, and yet there are few success stories of actually reducing corruption in a sustainable way.

This is why the church must help believers understand that salvation is not only about going to heaven but also about how we live on earth. Wesley taught that sanctified believers are called to be leaven in society, influencing every sphere with the values of the kingdom. This calls for courage, consistency, and a vision of holiness that is public and prophetic.

As several African theologians have emphasized, the continent's most pressing need is not merely an increase in the number of professing Christians but a transformation of society through the lived application of Christian ethics in both private and public spheres. As Kwame Bediako argued, "Christianity in Africa will be judged by its public significance."[14] Similarly, Kä Mana underscored the necessity of forming "a moral and spiritual foundation capable of addressing the crises of leadership, corruption, and injustice" in African societies.[15] Tite Tiénou also advocates for a holistic gospel that speaks to every dimension

13. See Dunning 1988 and 1991.

14. Bediako 1995, 9.

15. Mana 2002, 83.

of life, asserting that authentic Christian mission in Africa must shape both personal discipleship and social responsibility.[16] Together, these voices call for a form of Christianity that does not retreat from the public square but rather embodies ethical integrity, justice, and compassion in the face of systemic challenges.

The church's task, then, is to form disciples who are ready for public holiness. This includes teaching accountability, cultivating ethical awareness, challenging tribal and political loyalties that compromise integrity, and supporting those who suffer for doing right. As believers live with gospel conviction, institutions can be gradually reformed and reshaped.

The Role of the Spirit in Sustaining Holiness

Any call to holiness—especially in the face of entrenched corruption—would be overwhelming if it relied solely on human willpower. But the good news of the gospel is this: the call to live holy lives is matched by the gift of the Holy Spirit, who empowers believers to live in ways they never could on their own. Holiness is not human achievement; it is grace at work through the indwelling Spirit of God.

As Paul writes, "It is God who is at work in you, enabling you both to will and to work for his good pleasure" (Phil. 2:13). The Spirit not only convicts of sin but also reshapes desires, renews minds, and strengthens character. In a world where corruption often feels normal—or even necessary to survive—the Spirit forms an alternative vision of life marked by truth, justice, and sacrificial love.

The early church in Acts was born in a context of political oppression and economic disparity. Yet this Spirit-empowered community stood out for its boldness, generosity, and moral in-

16. Tiénou 2004.

tegrity. They did not merely preach holiness; they lived it, even under threat. The Spirit enabled them to confront injustice, share possessions, speak truth to power, and remain faithful amid persecution.

This same Spirit continues to empower the church today. Believers are not called to resist corruption by gritting their teeth—they are called to walk in the Spirit, to cultivate the fruit of the Spirit (Gal. 5:22-23), and to rely on the Spirit's guidance in all aspects of life. The church shaped by the gospel and endowed by the Spirit of God is expected to have an ethical influence on the life of the people.

This has radical implications for how Christians engage society. A Spirit-filled believer is not simply an honest person but a person on fire with God's love, equipped to challenge dishonesty, advocate for justice, and model integrity. The Spirit does not remove us from the world but sends us into it, just as Jesus prayed: "As you have sent me into the world, so I have sent them into the world" (John 17:18).

To resist corruption in sustained ways requires more than conviction—it requires spiritual empowerment, communal support, and daily renewal. The Spirit is not a luxury for elite Christians; the Holy Spirit is the essential resource for every believer seeking to live faithfully in a compromised world. When the church teaches people to rely on the Spirit and makes space for his work, it becomes a community marked by courage, purity, and resilient hope.

A Call to Courage and Hopeful Resistance

In societies where corruption is systemic and often normalized, standing for righteousness can be costly. Some lose jobs, others face harassment or isolation, and in some cases, lives are endangered. In such contexts, resisting corruption requires not only moral clarity but spiritual courage—a willingness to suffer for righteousness, anchored in the hope that God's justice will ultimately prevail.

The biblical narrative offers countless examples of such courageous faith. Daniel refused to compromise in Babylon. Esther risked her life to speak truth in the royal court. John the Baptist denounced the immorality of political leaders and paid with his life. Jesus himself was crucified by corrupt religious and political powers, yet his resurrection vindicated the way of righteousness and revealed the futility of evil.

These stories serve as more than history—they are testimonies to the reality that God honors those who walk in faithful resistance. As Jesus declared, "Blessed are those who are persecuted for righteousness' sake, for theirs is the kingdom of heaven" (Matt. 5:10, NKJV). Those who stand for truth may suffer in the present, but they participate in the coming kingdom, where justice will roll down like waters.

This is the kind of hopeful resistance (including choosing faithfulness over convenience or reward) the church must nurture—not rooted in bitterness or outrage, but in Spirit-empowered faithfulness, reflecting the character of God in the midst of a broken world. Such witness demands courage, vision, and costly love. But it also includes constructive engagement. Believers are called not only to denounce evil but to be redemptive.

The church has a role to play in this wounded world—to give biblical interpretations on moral issues, especially those related to corruption. This means forming a new generation of disciples and leaders who are not only spiritually mature but culturally discerning and ethically courageous. Ministerial training must go beyond pragmatism and focus on producing pastors and scholars who are prophetic voices—people who "prepare the way of the Lord" (Luke 3:4) by living truthfully and boldly, deeply rooted in Scripture and the gospel.

Such courage does not arise from human strength. It flows from the Spirit's sanctifying presence, from knowing that we do not stand alone. We are surrounded by "so great a cloud of witnesses" (Heb. 12:1), and we follow a Savior who bore the cross and conquered the grave. This resurrection hope empowers believers to persevere even when corruption seems overwhelming.

Hopeful resistance is not naive optimism—it is eschatological faith. It looks beyond the present darkness to the coming reign of Christ. It clings to the promise that "your labor in the Lord is not in vain" (1 Cor. 15:58, NIV) and that no act of faithful witness is ever wasted.

Conclusion: Proclaiming and Embodying the Gospel of Holiness in a Corrupt World

The church today stands at a crossroads. In a world where corruption is often normalized—even expected—the temptation to conform is strong. Yet the call of the gospel is unmistakable: "Be holy, for I am holy" (1 Pet. 1:16). This holiness is not an escape from the world but a bold witness within it—a life marked by truth, compassion, justice, and unshakable faithfulness to Christ.

Throughout this chapter, we have affirmed that the biblical vision of salvation is not limited to personal forgiveness but encompasses the transformation of persons, communities, and systems. Salvation is God's work of reclaiming all that has been distorted by sin, including the social and institutional structures that shape human life. When rightly understood, salvation is the antidote to corruption—not only because it deals with guilt but because it restores moral vision and renews moral power.

Salvation is not merely about escaping judgment but about being filled with love and empowered for holy living. Holiness is not just a set of rules but the renewal of the image of God in us—an image marked by God's holiness; holiness is about reflecting the very character of God to those around us.

To confront corruption, the church must do more than lament its spread. It must proclaim the gospel of grace that leads to repentance and radical change. And that call for repentance and change may well include people who are part of our worshipping communities. It must disciple believers to live with holy integrity in every vocation and relationship. It must equip them to stand firm in difficult contexts, supported by the power of the Holy Spirit and the strength of Christian community.

This work will not be easy. The forces of corruption are entrenched, complex, and often spiritual. But as people of the resurrection, we do not work in despair. We work in hope—believing that light overcomes darkness, that holiness is stronger than compromise, and that the gospel still changes lives. As Archbishop Desmond Tutu once said, "Goodness is stronger than evil; / Love is stronger than hate; / Light is stronger than darkness; / Life is stronger than death."[17]

Well over a century ago, Tyerman quotes John Wesley as having declared, "Give me one hundred preachers who fear nothing but sin and desire nothing but God, and . . . such alone will shake the gates of hell, and set up the kingdom of heaven upon earth."[18] That is the kind of courage and clarity the church needs today—not self-righteousness, but Spirit-empowered holiness.

Let the church be that holy people. Let it preach salvation as transformation. Let it stand against corruption—not with anger or arrogance, but with grace, truth, and sacrificial love. Let it declare with its life: There is a better way. There is a Savior who

---

17. Tutu 1995, 80.
18. Tyerman 1872, 632.

not only forgives but restores; not only justifies but sanctifies; not only saves souls but renews creation.

May we live as citizens of that kingdom—transformed by grace, walking in the light, and bringing the hope of holiness to a broken and corrupt world.

FIVE

JESUS, THE MESSIAH, THE SON OF GOD

1 JOHN 1:1-4, 7

The Early Church's Crossroads

Who is Jesus? It is a question echoed through the centuries, debated in councils, preached from pulpits, and whispered in the quiet of individual hearts. But this isn't merely an academic query for theologians. For followers of Christ, understanding Jesus's true identity—who he is, fully God and fully human—is not just a matter of correct belief; it is the very foundation of how we live, how we worship, and how we navigate the complexities of our faith in the world. As we turn to the first letter of John, we encounter a community wrestling with this exact question, discovering timeless truths for our own journey.

John addresses a Johannine community of believers confronting significant theological tensions. The Johannine community (church) was grappling with emerging heterodox interpretations concerning the nature of Jesus Christ. Some tendencies overemphasized his divinity at the expense of his humanity, while others exaggerated his humanity to the detriment of his divine identity. These theological deviations were more than academic; they threatened the foundation of the church's faith and practice.

Imagine driving on a two-lane road with lines on either side. If you drift too far to the left (like *only* seeing Jesus as human), you end up in the ditch. If you swerve too far to the right (like *only* seeing him as divine and not truly human), you also end up off the road. Staying centered on the road between the lines symbolizes understanding Jesus correctly as both fully God and fully human—that's the path John invites the church to stay on.

John writes to keep the church centered on this correct understanding of Jesus. The balance between fully God and fully human is not optional; it is foundational. The church must accurately understand Jesus Christ's person and nature, since orthopraxy (right living) flows directly from orthodoxy (right belief). A clear comprehension of Jesus Christ's person and nature is essential.

John's concern echoes what modern theologian Richard Bauckham emphasizes when he argues that New Testament Christology is best understood as placing Jesus within the unique divine identity.[1] "The inclusion of Jesus in the unique identity of God is precisely in the context of his humiliation and death. God's identity is now to be known in Jesus' human life and especially in his cross."[2] Jesus is not merely God's agent but fully shares in the divine name and prerogatives. This theological framework is essential for safeguarding the integrity of Christian worship and discipleship.

It is not surprising that John begins his first letter with a theological affirmation (who God is—specifically, who Jesus is) and ties this with an ethical injunction (how we should live in the light

1. Bauckham 2008.
2. Bauckham 1998, 30.

of it). This establishes the principle that Christian conduct derives organically from foundational Christian belief. Specifically, orthopraxy is predicated upon orthodoxy, with Christology serving as the essential cornerstone. The epistle's central proclamation, its *kerygma,* revolves around the life-imparting gospel intrinsically linked to the person of Jesus Christ. Living in accordance with divine truth necessitates a correct apprehension of him.

The core message that John shares is incredibly good news! Through Jesus, God offers us amazing gifts: life connected to God, a relationship with God the Father and Jesus his Son, and with each other as followers of Christ. This community is vital for our growth in Christ and the complete joy that comes from being right with God and walking in God's light. First John centers on the unique self-disclosure of God mediated through the historical person of Jesus (1:1-3).

Confronting the specific Christological deviations, John meticulously constructs a balanced formulation. To counter potential docetic leanings, perhaps influenced by Hellenistic dualism emphasizing spirit over matter, John appeals to scriptural traditions and apostolic testimony underscoring the manifest reality of Jesus's human life, suffering, and death (e.g., John 10:25-38; 1 John 1:7*b*-9; 2:2, 6, 12; 3:5, 8, 16; 4:2, 9-10, 17). Conversely, addressing tendencies possibly rooted in a Jewish milieu inclined to exaggerate Jesus's humanity, John asserts Christ's preexistence, inherent holiness, purity, and future eschatological return in glory (e.g., 1 John 2:13-14, 20, 28-29; 3:2-3, 5, 7; 5:20*b*).[3]

3. See Smalley 1991.

Staying Centered: The Incarnational Reality

First John presents a Christology that maintains the essential tension:[4] Jesus Christ is concurrently one with God and one with humanity. See 1:1-4, especially verses 1-2; 2:22-23; 5:1*a*:

> We declare to you what was from the beginning, what we have heard, what we have seen with our eyes, what we have looked at and touched with our hands, concerning the word of life—this life was revealed, and we have seen it and testify to it and declare to you the eternal life that was with the Father and was revealed to us. (1:1-2)

> Who is the liar but the one who denies that Jesus is the Christ? This is the antichrist, the one who denies the Father and the Son. No one who denies the Son has the Father; everyone who confesses the Son has the Father also. (2:22-23)

> Everyone who believes that Jesus is the Christ has been born of God. (5:1*a*)

So, why is the prologue (1:1-4) salient? Because John emphasizes how the first apostles (the apostles' witness) saw, heard, and touched Jesus—"the word of life." This person was simultaneously eternal and yet historically manifest, perceptible through sensory experience ("seen," "heard," "touched"). This incarnational reality, the tangible manifestation of the invisible God through the Son, is core. Believing Jesus is fully God and fully human, both at the same time, is nonnegotiable for John!

Ultimately, this carefully balanced Christology possesses profound soteriological implications. John inextricably links eternal life to a relationship with the Son: "God gave us eternal

4. This reminder by Bauckham (2008, 3-7) is essential. The recognition of Jesus's inclusion in the divine identity is not a postbiblical development, but the basis from which classical Christology develops.

life, and this life is in his Son. Whoever has the Son has life; whoever does not have the Son of God does not have life" (5:11-12). Thus, adherence to a correct, apostolic understanding of the person of Jesus Christ is presented not merely as a matter of doctrinal precision but as essential for participation in the divine life offered by God.

The Enduring Journey: Our Present-Day Challenge

The question of who Jesus is continues to be critical for the church today. The fundamental questions surrounding the full divinity and full humanity of Jesus Christ, as established by early church councils such as Nicaea and Chalcedon, remain vital to Christian theology. Yet in the twenty-first century, Christological inquiry is shaped by new concerns—relativism, pluralism, and the need for contextual expressions of faith. The key question, "Who is Jesus?" continues to resonate across cultures, inviting theologians to interpret and communicate Christ within the lived realities of diverse peoples.

One such contextual approach is African Christology, particularly the stream often described as "from below."[5] This model begins with human experience—specifically, the social, cultural, and political realities of African life—and moves toward affirming Jesus's divinity through that lens. It is incarnational, experiential, and deeply rooted in the African worldview. Jesus is first encountered as an ancestor, fellow sufferer, a healer, a liberator, and an elder—one who deeply understands and engages with the

5. Christology "from below" and "from above" refers to the method by which we come to think of the doctrine of Christ as fully human and fully God. Many scholars suggest that African theology in general is "from below"—implying that it begins with the emphasis on the humanity of Christ in contrast with Western Christology, which has often started "from above"—emphasizing Christ's divine nature and then connecting it to his humanity.

realities of life. Thus, in general, it is believed that many contemporary Christian intellectuals in Africa are much preoccupied with inculturation.[6] From there, the discussion moves toward affirming Jesus's divinity, always grounded in real, lived experiences within the contexts of traditional African worldviews.

African Christology "from below" might include the following:

- *Jesus as Healer.* Healing holds a central place in African life. Theologians often present Jesus as a divine healer who accompanies the sick and marginalized. His ministry connects with African spiritual practices and responses to crisis, making him immediately relatable.
- *Jesus as Liberator.* Within histories marked by colonialism, apartheid, and systemic oppression, Jesus is seen as a liberator who stands with the oppressed. His ministry is revolutionary and prophetic, confronting injustice and echoing the resistance movements within African history.
- *Jesus as Elder.* In African communities, elders are respected leaders and custodians of wisdom. Jesus, as the divine Elder, offers guidance, justice, and peace, resonating with the structure and values of African communal life.
- *Jesus as Ancestor.* In African traditional religions, ancestors mediate between the divine and the living. Jesus is interpreted as the ultimate Ancestor—not just a mediator, but the source of divine presence. This often reduces Jesus to one among many African spiritual entities. Gift Mtukwa has done a great deal of work to call on the followers of Christ in Africa to cut ties with the cult of the

6. Isichei 1995.

ancestors or anything that competes for the allegiance to Christ alone.[7]

Ancestor veneration, as practiced within the framework of African traditional religion, is fundamentally incompatible with biblical Christianity, since it undermines the exclusive mediatory role of Jesus Christ affirmed in Scripture. The New Testament presents Christ as the sole and sufficient Mediator between God and humanity (1 Tim. 2:5; Heb. 9:15), rendering any appeal to ancestral intermediaries theologically redundant and doctrinally problematic. While the African emphasis on community and remembrance of the dead resonates with the Christian doctrine of the communion of saints, biblical faith is opposed to invoking the dead (Lev. 19:31; Deut. 18:10-13). Accordingly, African theological reflection must distinguish between culturally meaningful remembrance and religious practices that contradict the Christocentric foundation of Christian worship and soteriology.[8]

Cultural Detours: The Risks of Contextualization

While contextualization aims to benefit the context by presenting the Christian gospel in ways that resonate deeply within a specific cultural setting, using familiar frameworks—local customs, symbols, stories, philosophies—to explain Christian truths, it is not without risks. The primary danger is syncretism.[9] Syncre-

7. Mtukwa 2014.

8. Mtukwa 2014.

9. "Where Christianity is professed, there is a constant dialectic arising from its relationship with the cultural presuppositions and practices of the cultures where it is located. Christianity came to sub-Saharan Africa in European cultural packaging, and contextualization, as we have seen, has been a major concern of Africa's theologians. However, clearly there is a point where contextualization becomes syncretism, and Christian content is eroded, losing 'the

tism is the blending or merging of different, often incompatible, beliefs and practices. In this context, it refers to mixing traditional, non-Christian cultural or religious beliefs with the Christian faith in ways that might compromise orthodox theology—that is, distort or contradict the core, historically accepted doctrines of Christianity (such as the nature of God, the person of Christ, and salvation). This is not just a theoretical danger; it is often a practical reality well documented in several scholarly works.

Christology (the doctrine concerning who Jesus is) is a major area of concern. When trying to make Jesus relatable within a culture (e.g., portraying him like a local hero, ancestor figure, or wise teacher), there's a risk of overemphasizing his humanity to the point that his divinity gets obscured or downplayed. While Jesus's true humanity is a vital part of orthodox belief (he is fully God and fully human), stressing one aspect to the neglect of the other leads to an incomplete or distorted picture.

If Jesus's divinity is overshadowed, he risks being reduced to merely a "cultural symbol" or a "moral example." While he *is* an example, he is fundamentally more than that. This reduction neglects his unique and essential roles as the Messiah of God, the promised deliverer and King; the One who reconciles us to God, the unique Mediator who bridges the gap caused by sin; our Savior, the One who saves from sin and its consequences; the Son of God, he who possesses the unique relationship with the Father, affirming his divine nature.

While I specifically highlighted issues with which the Christian community wrestles in Africa, the core challenge resonates across all cultural settings. Whenever we engage in interpreting who Jesus is, especially when seeking to address contemporary

conforming of a Church's life to standards outside itself, standards which may cut across everyone's culture pattern' [Walls 1976, 188]" (Isichei 1995, 4).

life issues, we encounter the same "essential tension" faced by the Johannine community. We must diligently strive, as John did, to maintain a holistic understanding of the person and nature of Jesus Christ, guarding against distortions.

The Path of Orthopraxy: Belief Guiding Life

Our lived faith, our orthopraxy, inevitably flows from our Christological understanding, our orthodoxy. Therefore, how we articulate Jesus's identity in relation to our context directly impacts how we live. Recognizing this, the effort to make the gospel culturally relevant and comprehensible is profoundly important—indeed, it is a necessity. Christianity has always, by its very nature, engaged with diverse cultures to make the good news comprehensible and transformative. It's not a question of whether to contextualize, but how to do it faithfully, ensuring the core tenets of Christian orthodoxy remain uncompromised. As Dean Flemming powerfully argues in *Contextualization in the New Testament: Patterns for Theology and Mission,* contextualization is "the dynamic and comprehensive process by which the gospel is incarnated within a concrete historical or cultural situation . . . in such a way that the gospel both comes to authentic expression in the local context and at the same time prophetically transforms the context. Contextualization seeks to enable the people of God to live out the gospel in obedience to Christ within their own cultures and circumstances."[10] The task, then, is to discern wise and biblically sound patterns for expressing the timeless truth of Christ in culturally relevant ways, without ever watering down or distorting the "Word of life" itself.[11]

10. Flemming 2005, 19.

11. See Flemming 2005. Throughout his work, Dean Flemming demonstrates that faithful witness to Jesus must attend carefully to biblical testimony

Yet, as the potential for syncretism and imbalance warned against in 1 John illustrates, this process requires profound care. An overemphasis on Jesus's humanity for the sake of relevance can inadvertently obscure his essential divinity, potentially reducing him to less than the Scriptures proclaim: the Messiah, the Son of God, the unique Reconciler and Savior. Faithful contextualization must balance relevance with unwavering faithfulness to the core apostolic doctrine of the fully divine, fully human Christ.

Of course, the method employed—whether "from above" or "from below"—can yield valuable insights about Christ, who is fully God and fully human. However, it is essential to recognize that "historical research is a purely human endeavour that can lead us to the threshold of faith. But it cannot take us over the threshold! Our own reasoning does not bring us all the way to faith. Faith is the gift of God. Our own insight . . . may help us, but it cannot be the basis of our faith."[12]

Thomas Noble offers a helpful insight:

> Christology does not begin, therefore, with either of the "two"—either "from above," that is, with the deity, or "from below," that is, with the historical humanity. Our faith only begins at the moment when we kneel before Christ and confess, "My Lord and my God!" Faith begins with the recognition of the One-in-two. The "given" is . . . the proclamation in the Gospel that in Jesus Christ, these "two" are "one." To recognize and know Jesus Christ as Lord is therefore not our own achievement or insight. It is only when the Spirit gives us the ability to recognize him as Lord that we know

---

while also engaging the concrete questions and concerns of particular cultural settings. Such engagement reflects the incarnational nature of the gospel rather than theological compromise.

12. Noble 2025b, 169.

who Jesus is. It is only by grace. In other words, theology is not intellectually proving the Christian faith to be true. It is rather "faith seeking understanding."[13]

Stay on the Path

As already implied, 1 John was written in the context of polarization, which was widening the gap between different theological perspectives within the community of believers, resulting in division. Amid this, John offers a path forward. He addresses the issues by calling for unity while pointing to the hope we have in Jesus, the Messiah, the incarnate God, and the One who can atone for our sins. It sounds as if John is saying to us today that in a complex and polarized world, we must put our full trust in Jesus the Messiah, the Son of God—he is "the path" we must stay on.

A few years ago, I ventured with friends on a backpacking trip to Oregon's breathtaking Pacific Crest Trail (PCT), beginning at Fish Lake and ending at Mazama Village. The majestic mountains, cascading waterfalls, lakes, and diverse fellow hikers made it an awe-inspiring journey.

During this backpacking trip, my friends and I faced an unexpected challenge. Simply put, "We got lost," and we had no means of communication because there was no cell phone connection. I like to think that this was no one's fault, but rather it was caused by previous years' forest fires, which had obscured the trail and camping areas. We were a group of six, but only four got lost—two were ahead of us. Our friends who were ahead of us, recognizing that the trail was not visible, left us a note along the way to guide us. It was cryptic, and we couldn't decipher their instructions. It read, "Turn here .4 miles." Where? To the right or the left? Four preachers tried to exegete the text (the orig-

13. Noble 2025b, 169.

inal text) with no success. We were stranded in an area seemingly untouched by humans for a long time; we were exhausted and running low on water. It was a frightening situation.

Fortunately, we stumbled upon a small creek, where we decided to camp for the night and continue our search for an escape the next day. Our salvation came in the form of the All-Trails app. We decided to review previous maps and trails we had downloaded on the app, and luckily, it showed us how far off course we were. It began guiding us back to the trail, ultimately leading us to safety.

When we regained cell phone reception and contacted the other group, two nights had passed since they last saw or heard from us. They had already reported us missing, and word had spread among hikers that four men were lost. They had provided accurate descriptions of us (one tall black man and three white guys), so as we headed toward Crater Lake, we encountered several hikers who recognized us as the lost men. We were on the right track, but many of them took the time to give us directions and to assure us that we were on the right path. Often, their instructions included this advice: "Stay on the trail; you'll reach your destination—Crater Lake." You see, one of the reasons we got lost is that in our attempt to find the path, we veered too far away from the trail. I have learned that it does not take long to get lost when you start wandering around!

I have thought about this adventure as I reflect on how the church today is grappling with living out its faith in the world's complexities. We find in 1 John a reminder that believers throughout history have always grappled with the integration of gospel teachings and ethical considerations into their daily lives. Early Christians faced similar dilemmas, with some (Jewish Christians) adhering to Jewish traditions—Judaism's laws and rules—as a standard for Christianity. In contrast, others (known as Hellenistic Christians) struggled to reconcile the concept of an incarnate God with their understanding of the material world. There were other issues, such as false teaching and persecution. As you read through 1 John, it will be evident that the believers faced the risk of adopting heterodox (heterogeneous) beliefs, teetering between excessively robust and overly feeble Christological stances.

My hope is that the church today will heed John's encouragement to remain faithful to its walk with and in Christ. John's way of saying "Here is the trail" aims to strengthen the faith and

My grandmother suffered for years with leprosy. During the civil war in Mozambique, medical help was scarce, and she endured great pain. Yet through it all, her life radiated joy in Christ. She often reminded me that there is a difference between knowing about God and truly knowing God. Through her walk and fellowship with Christ, she had come to know him personally, and her life reflected godliness and full consecration.

One day, she told me words I will never forget: "Nothing can separate me from God's presence. Even in this body, broken by illness, his presence dwells here, and his glory shines through." Her body bore the marks of suffering, yet her faith revealed the reality John describes: "We declare to you what we have seen and heard so that you also may have fellowship with us; and truly our fellowship is with the Father and with his Son Jesus Christ" (1 John 1:3, NRSVA).

Her testimony reminds us that fellowship with Christ is not abstract knowledge but living communion. And even in weakness, the glory of God shines through.

determination of the believers, encouraging them to embrace the apostolic gospel unwaveringly. To fulfill this purpose, John urges the church to develop a solid comprehension of Jesus's essence, of who he is, through the power of the Spirit, to live in accordance with the gospel of Jesus Messiah.

The life that Jesus came to give us transcends the brokenness and evil that permeate our world. In taking on human form, Jesus, the incarnate God, came to restore our relationship and fellowship with God and, as 1 John so powerfully reminds us, one another. He revealed that God is the true source of life, the One who breathes newness into our weary souls. This divine life not only enables us to live without succumbing to sin, but it also empowers us to resist the snares of evil. Through Jesus, God has made possible a transformative change within us, a change that allows us to rise above the limitations of this world.

In essence, Jesus is not just a teacher or prophet but the very source of life itself—he is God (one with God and one with humanity). He offers himself to us as the means of reconciling with God.

As Dennis Kinlaw insightfully affirms, the only hope for genuine human salvation lies in the incarnation—God's holy love entering our humanity.[14] In Jesus, the eternal Son of God took on our nature, becoming fully human while remaining fully divine. This profound act was possible because of who God is—a triune, relational being—and because human beings were created for personal relationship with God. Unlike other religious systems that rely on human effort to reach the divine, Christianity proclaims that salvation begins with God's initiative and is sustained by his grace. In Christ, God himself makes atonement for our sins. This is the heart of the gospel: salvation is not achieved

14. Kinlaw 2005, 132.

through human striving but is received through the self-giving love of God.

By taking on human form as the visible manifestation of the invisible God, Jesus becomes tangible to our senses, making God's essence more accessible to humanity. This profound message invites us to a journey of deep reflection and exploration of Jesus's nature and how this is to be lived out in our complex world. It is not just about acknowledging these truths intellectually; it is about accepting them personally and corporately and experiencing them firsthand. This means that simply knowing about Jesus and his holiness isn't enough; we need to engage with Jesus in a real and personal way. We are called to become who we are in Christ through the Spirit.

Through Jesus, God's message and salvation are accessible to humanity. It is no longer something that is distant (based on rules that are hard to follow in our own power and strength, a vision for deliverance, etc.); it is a present, life-giving relationship that enables those who believe to know and grow in understanding God's way of life. Life in God is about having a deep, unending relationship with God. Hearing, seeing, touching, and proclaiming are experiential, and this is vital for any genuine and lasting response to the gospel. The historical life that was and is in God has now been revealed in word and person—it has become visible and knowable.

Jesus, who has come as one with God and one with humankind, is God's self-disclosure in time and space. We must meet him in time and space in our own lives, both personally and as a holy people. The result is/will be that what was true from eternity has been, and continues to be, gradually and actually disclosed (breaking into our world) and personally (individually and in community) experienced in time and space.

Encounter with the Messiah must be followed by the embodiment of a new life, personally and as the body of Christ. Like John, we bear witness to the eternal life that has been revealed to us: "The life appeared; we have seen it and testify to it, and we proclaim to you the eternal life, which was with the Father and has appeared to us" (1 John 1:2, NIV). We acknowledge that God is the wellspring of our existence, sustaining us from our inception to our current moment and for eternity.

The life God gives is not passive; it is marked by activity, light, joy, order, and purpose. It is a transformative life that God instills within us, crafting new hearts filled with his glory and righteousness, upholding and empowering us to embody this life-changing essence in our world.

Fellowship as Compass: Navigating the Path Together

Furthermore, John tells us that such life is lived in fellowship with one another. Fellowship involves sharing life, learning from each other, loving, listening, and growing together. It also requires humility and patience with one another and even, or perhaps especially, forgiveness of one another.

The backpacking story is a beautiful example of how fellowship can transcend differences and create a sense of unity. People from all walks of life come together on the trail, sharing a common goal and supporting one another through challenges. Even when faced with setbacks, like getting lost, the group finds strength in their camaraderie. This sense of fellowship extends beyond the trail, as strangers and fellow hikers offer help and encouragement.

Fellowship (Gk., *koinōnia*) is vital for the church. It is about sharing, hospitality, caring, patience, and reminding one another to stay on the path. Just as hikers support each other on the trail,

Christians support one another on their spiritual journey. We are on the trail together!

First John 1:7 is significant: "But if we walk in the light as he himself is in the light, we have fellowship with one another, and the blood of Jesus his Son cleanses us from all sin." Christian life is not solitary; it is communal. Fellowship (Gk., *koinōnia*) is central. It means sharing life, practicing hospitality, offering forgiveness, and bearing one another's burdens. Kent Brower notes, "The identity of God as light holds profound implications for the life of Christian discipleship. . . . The holy community . . . mirrors God's holy nature."[15] To walk in the light is to live in obedience, not just to rules but to the character of God as revealed in Christ. Therefore, those who claim to walk in the light cannot simultaneously embrace the darkness.

John emphasizes that the holy community's life is rooted in a relationship with Christ. Thus, knowing, abiding, and remaining in Christ—in *koinōnia* with Christ and centered in the love of God—forms the foundation of this fellowship. This mutual participation in Christ and with fellow believers is far more than a natural affinity; it stems from their shared participation in the very being of the Triune God.

Walking in the light requires obedience to God, not merely adhering to a set of rules but emulating God's loving character and the obedience of the Son. This obedience is not a passive acceptance of Christ's actions but an active participation in his obedience, empowered by the Spirit's indwelling. John links walking, obedience, abiding, and love in one statement: "By this we may know that we are in him: whoever says, 'I abide in him,' ought to walk in the same way as he walked" (2:5-6).

15. Brower 2014, 135.

Obedience to the word, particularly the great commands to love God and neighbor, is essential for walking in the light. John boldly asserts that whoever obeys God's words truly embodies the love of God (v. 5). Walking in the light is synonymous with abiding in God. It manifests as mirroring God's love within the community and toward the world.

True holiness cannot be confined to individual spirituality. It is also the presence of love, demonstrated in acts of love within the fellowship of the church and toward others.

As we live in fellowship, God continues to pour his life into us. We learn to hear, see, and touch God in time and space through our shared experiences. While fellowship does not guarantee perfection, it acknowledges Jesus's power to transform us into his likeness.

In fellowship with one another, and with God, we learn to trust Jesus with our lives. As we respond to his transformative work, we experience and witness the extraordinary redemptive and restorative work of God in us and through us.

Our backpacking story reminded me of this: strangers became helpers; fellow travelers gave guidance. The church is called to be such people, walking together in the light. Walking in the light is walking in love. It is abiding in Christ.

The danger of polarization lies in the tendency to stray from the true image of God, as revealed by Jesus Messiah, the Son of God. Following John's admonition, let us prioritize a return to the centrality of Christ, the incarnate and atoning Messiah.

Conclusion

The message of 1 John is as relevant now as ever. In a world of theological confusion and cultural complexity, the church must anchor itself in the full confession of Jesus Christ as fully God and fully human.

This Christological center is not a doctrinal luxury but a salvific necessity. Our life, fellowship, holiness, and mission flow from it.

We must heed John's call to stay on the path: to confess Jesus as the incarnate Son, to live in fellowship, to walk in the light, and to become living witnesses of the eternal life that has appeared among us.

Let us, therefore, with the Spirit's help, proclaim and embody Jesus, the Messiah, the Son of God. May we do so with theological clarity and cultural humility, holding fast to the truth that Jesus is fully God and fully human. Let us remember that our lived holiness flows from our Christology and that faithful contextualization allows the gospel to speak clearly and powerfully into every culture without compromise. As we journey together in fellowship, walking in the light, may we reflect the love, truth, and transformative power of Jesus Christ in a world longing for redemption. May our churches, our communities, and our lives bear witness to the eternal life that has been revealed in the Son.

PARTNERS IN GRACE: LIVING THE GOSPEL TOGETHER

PHILIPPIANS 1:3-11

When Paul wrote to the Philippians, he was writing not just to a group of believers but to cherished partners—people who had walked with him, prayed for him, supported his ministry, and suffered for the sake of the gospel. His opening words are far more than a polite greeting—they are a profound affirmation of shared grace and active participation in God's redemptive mission.

Paul's joy is unmistakable. His gratitude flows from the knowledge that this church is not passively observing the gospel—they are actively living it. They are his coworkers in Christ. He writes, "I thank my God every time I remember you . . . because of your sharing in the gospel from the first day until now" (Phil. 1:3, 5, NRSVA).

This opening prayer captures one of the deepest truths of the Christian life: The Christian life is not a solitary endeavor; we are not called to be isolated individuals striving to please God on our own. We are the body of Christ, formed and sustained by God's grace and sent into the world to live the gospel together.

This chapter explores the implications of that shared calling—what it means to live as gospel partners, grow in love and wisdom, and persevere in the hope that God is at work among us. As we reflect on Philippians 1:3-11, may we be reminded that we do not walk this path alone. We walk together, as partners in grace.

What Does It Mean to Share in the Gospel?

"Sharing in the gospel" (Phil. 1:5, NRSVA; Gk., *koinōnia eis to euangelion*) means living as an active participant in the mission of God. This phrase implies far more than intellectual agreement or passive support. It conveys a profound sense of partnership, solidarity, and shared vocation. The church is not a mere recipient of the gospel but a co-laborer in it, called to embody the gospel through word, deed, and faithful presence in the world.

This was true for the Philippians in the first century, and it remains true for us today. To share in the gospel is to join God's mission wherever we are—in prayer, generosity, solidarity, and suffering. The Philippians demonstrate this partnership through their intercessory prayer, financial generosity, relational solidarity, and readiness to suffer alongside Paul. Their example reminds us that gospel participation is not an abstract idea but a lived reality that defines who we are and how we live. It is both a spiritual identity and a concrete missional practice. It is incarnational in nature—we are called not just to preach Christ but to live Christ in the world.

As scholars have noted, this incarnational understanding of mission lies at the heart of the New Testament vision. N. T. Wright insightfully observes: "The gospel of God, today and tomorrow as in Paul's day . . . must become, as it did in Jesus, flesh and blood. That which was unveiled before an unprepared world in Jesus Christ must be unveiled again and again, as those who believe in Jesus Christ live by the Spirit and, in life as well as in word, announce the gospel to the world."[1]

This incarnational calling reflects the *missio Dei*—the mission of the Triune God to redeem and restore all creation. As Dean Flemming emphasizes, the church's mission flows from the very nature of God.[2] It is God who sends, and the church who goes. Our participation is rooted in our fellowship with Christ and empowered by the Spirit.

Paul reminds the Corinthians, "God is faithful; by him you were called into the fellowship of his Son, Jesus Christ our Lord" (1 Cor. 1:9, NRSVA). Similarly, the apostle John affirms, "Truly our fellowship is with the Father and with his Son Jesus Christ" (1 John 1:3). This language of fellowship conveys more than spiritual intimacy; it speaks to a covenantal relationship initiated by God's faithfulness and sustained through our responsive faithfulness. As James D. G. Dunn highlights (1998), faith for Paul was not a mere act of belief or verbal confession; it was an embodied, relational response, a life of loyalty and obedience shaped by union with Christ.[3]

To share in the gospel, then, is to participate in this dynamic relationship with God and with one another. It is both relational and transformational. The gospel is not proclaimed by words alone but demonstrated through a way of life aligned with the character of Christ. Dunn's analysis, rooted in the "New Perspective" on Paul, helps us see that justification initiates a lifelong journey of covenantal fidelity—a participation "in Christ" that reshapes how we live, love, and serve. Faith becomes visible in

1. N. T. Wright 2014, 199.
2. Flemming 2013, 17.
3. Dunn 1998.

In 1907, two young missionaries, Harmon Schmelzenbach and his wife, Lula Glatzel, boarded a ship to Africa with little more than faith and a calling. They carried the prayers and support of churches back home and the conviction that "Africa must hear the gospel."

In Eswatini, they faced sickness, hostility, and even the grief of burying three infants. Still, they persevered. Harmon began work on a church building even before any converts had come. Day after day, he prayed there, trusting God to bring people. In time, a small group gathered, and soon those first believers became partners, praying and working with them to spread the gospel.

What began with a handful of faithful people has grown into nearly a million believers across Africa today. Their story echoes Paul's words to the Philippians: "I thank my God every time I remember you . . . because of your sharing in the gospel from the first day until now" (1:3, 5, NRSVA). God's mission advances through such partnerships—those who send, those who go, and those who receive and carry the gospel forward, and the One who began this good work will surely bring it to completion.

acts of obedience, in Spirit-empowered living, and in the witness of a community formed by grace.

Christopher J. H. Wright expands this vision further by emphasizing the missional breadth of the gospel. He reminds us that the good news is not only personal but cosmic in scope: "The gospel must be big enough to encompass the whole of God's mission—and small enough to transform the life of every person who receives it."[4] In this light, faithfulness to Christ means embodying the gospel in our daily lives while participating in God's redemptive mission for the world.

This redemptive mission is not a side task of the church; it is our very identity. The church exists for the world—to be a sign, witness, and foretaste of God's kingdom. When we share in the gospel, we are not merely conveying information but bearing witness to the life, death, and resurrection of Jesus by becoming a people who live in the light of it.

To "share in the gospel," then, is to be co-missioned with Christ—to be a holy people formed by grace and sent in love. It means allowing our lives to become the canvas on which the good news of Jesus is seen, heard, and felt. It is not only something we do but who we are.

"The One Who Began a Good Work among You Will Bring It to Completion" (Phil. 1:6, NRSVA)

Sharing in the gospel is beautiful but also costly. Paul's words in Philippians 1:6 are both a reassurance and a declaration of hope: God, who initiated the work of salvation, will faithfully complete it. His confidence is not rooted in the Philippians' ability to remain faithful, but in God's covenantal faithfulness to bring to fulfillment what he has begun in them. This statement is a reminder that divine grace sustains the believer through every season of the journey.

The Greek construction in verse 6—*ho enarxamenos en hymin ergon agathon* (the one who began a good work in you)—emphasizes the divine initiative. God is the one who initiates the work of salvation in a believer's life, and this work is characterized by

4. C. Wright 2006, 129.

intentionality and grace. As Gordon Fee observes, Paul's focus is not on what God is doing through the Philippians, but on what he is doing in them—namely, their salvation in Christ.[5] This "good work" refers to their experience of and participation in the gospel, which is being lived out in their community. By affirming that God has both begun and will complete this saving work, Paul anticipates his later exhortation (2:12-13) that they live out their salvation, precisely because God continues to work within them. The phrase "will bring it to completion" (*epitelesei*) implies not merely survival but full maturity in Christ (cf. Rom. 8:29; Eph. 4:13).

In the context of Philippians, this confidence is especially poignant. Paul is writing from prison (Phil. 1:13-14), and the Philippians themselves appear to be facing some opposition (vv. 28-30). Yet Paul assures them that their faithfulness is not in vain. As Peter T. O'Brien notes, Paul's confidence is not rooted in the Philippians' own perseverance but in God's character and initiative.[6] The assurance of completion is grounded in God's unwavering commitment to his redemptive purpose and saving work among them.

Theologically, Philippians 1:6 affirms the doctrine of sanctification as both process and promise. God's grace transforms; this speaks to the hope of entire sanctification—not as a human achievement, but as the fulfillment of God's gracious work to conform us to the likeness of Christ (cf. 1 Thess. 5:23-24).

In practical terms, Paul's words offer hope for believers who feel discouraged, weary, or disillusioned. In a world where many Christians are tempted to give up because of secularism, injustice, moral failures, or personal suffering, Paul reminds us that God is not finished with us. His grace continues to work in

5. Fee 1995, 84-87.
6. O'Brien 1991.

hidden places, often beyond our perception. Christian confidence is not arrogance; it is faith in the God who has already acted in Jesus and who will complete what he has begun.

The promise of Philippians 1:6 also invites the church to persevere in mission. In places where the church is persecuted or marginalized, this verse becomes a lifeline. In contexts, for example, where believers may face resistance from cultural traditions, ancestral practices, or even state systems, the assurance that God will bring his work to completion sustains both individuals and communities in faithfulness. As Tite Tiénou has observed, Christian hope must be both "eschatological and ethical"—anchored in the coming kingdom but lived out through everyday holiness and public integrity.[7]

Furthermore, this verse challenges leaders and congregations not to measure success solely by visible outcomes. Faithfulness is sometimes quiet, even costly. But our task is to cooperate with God's grace, to walk in obedience, and to trust that he is shaping us—even when growth is slow or obscured by trials. This is the tension of the "already and not yet." God's kingdom has been inaugurated in Christ. The new creation has begun (2 Cor. 5:17). But until Christ returns, we live with our eyes fixed on him, trusting in his grace to sustain and complete what he has started.

Ultimately, Paul's declaration is a call to hope: hope that rests not in human strength, but in divine faithfulness. The same God who raised Jesus from the dead is at work in us, and he will not abandon his work. As we surrender to his purposes, we become living testimonies of God's transforming power.

7. See Tiénou 1990, 2004, 2006.

Love Abounding in Knowledge and Insight (Phil. 1:9-11)

Paul's prayer in Philippians 1:9-11 reflects his deep pastoral concern for the spiritual maturity of the church. He is not content with mere emotional affection among believers. Rather, he prays for a love that "may abound more and more in knowledge and depth of insight" (v. 9, NIV)—a love that is spiritually informed, ethically discerning, and rooted in a relationship with Christ.

The Greek term *agapē* refers to self-giving, covenantal love—the kind of love embodied in Christ and poured into our hearts through the Holy Spirit (Rom. 5:5). But this love, Paul insists, must not be blind or naive. It must abound in *epignōsis* (deep, experiential knowledge of God) and *aisthēsis* (moral and spiritual discernment) (Phil. 1:9). These are not abstract ideals; they are essential capacities for living the gospel faithfully in a complex and often deceptive world.

For Paul, knowledge is not simply intellectual mastery but relational fidelity and transformation. The knowledge of God Paul values is fundamentally relational—formed in obedience and faithfulness—and is the kind of knowledge that shapes ethical behavior, discernment, and love.

In other words, true love is not separate from wisdom—it is shaped by it. Christian love must be infused with a Spirit-enabled ability to discern rightly, to evaluate what truly matters, and to live accordingly. This aligns with Paul's intent when he prays that the Philippians would "discern what is best" (v. 10, NIV) or, as other translations put it, "approve what is excellent" (e.g., ESV).

Dean Flemming puts it this way: "Love without knowledge and insight can be permissive and morally flabby. . . . Paul is not so much praying for a more *intense* love as a more *intelligent* love. He desires for his Philippian friends a love that evidences a genuine experiential knowledge of God and a pattern of moral decisions that accord with God's will."[8] Gordon Fee echoes this concern, writing that "love that is not coupled with discernment may be kind but not necessarily good."[9] The integration of love and understanding is profoundly important. For Paul, love must be guided by discernment of God's purposes. This produces not merely proper emotions but faithful conduct. Genuine Christian maturity requires learning to love with wisdom, forming moral judgments shaped not by cultural expectations or personal preferences but by the mind of Christ. Paul's vision of love is therefore neither arbitrary nor subjective; it is ethically demanding, purposeful, and sustained by hope that shapes belief, practice, community, obedience, character, witness, perseverance, and faithfulness.

This kind of love is vital for Christian maturity, especially in a pluralistic age where not everything that appears good aligns with God's will. As Paul writes in Romans 12:2, believers must not be conformed to the world's patterns but be transformed through the renewing of their minds—so they can discern what is "good and acceptable and perfect." Discernment, in Paul's vision, is not about rigidity but about seeing the world through the lens of God's redeeming purposes.

The end goal of this discerning love, as Paul prays in Philippians 1:10-11, is that believers "may be pure and blameless for the day of Christ" and "filled with the fruit of righteousness that comes through Jesus Christ" (NIV). This vision of holiness is not a privatized, inward piety but a thoroughly ethical way of life that flows from participation in the gospel. As Dunn makes clear, Paul's theology never separates doctrine from practice; the indic-

8. Flemming 2009, 57.
9. Fee 1995, 85.

ative of salvation—God's initiating work in Christ—is the essential ground for the imperative of moral formation. Holiness, then, is the visible outworking of what God has already accomplished. It is lived through discernment, formed in love, and enabled by the Spirit. This "fruit of righteousness" reflects not merely moral effort but a Spirit-enabled conformity to the character of Christ, rooted in the "law of faith," "law of the Spirit," and "law of Christ."[10]

In this light, love becomes not only the aim but also the means of ethical transformation. For Paul, as Dunn argues, faith that trusts in God leads to obedience, the Spirit renews the heart and empowers right judgment, and Christ's example of self-giving love becomes the model for Christian conduct.[11] The righteousness that believers embody is not legalistic performance but the fulfillment of the law through Spirit-shaped love. Thus, Paul's prayer in Philippians is a plea for a life formed by theological ethics—a life where love abounds in knowledge and discernment, where believers become a living anticipation of the day of Christ, and where their conduct gives glory to God. Holiness is, therefore, neither abstract nor unattainable: it is the daily practice of becoming what we are in Christ.

Diane Leclerc, writing from a Wesleyan-Holiness perspective, deepens this theological insight: "Sanctification must be followed by a growing maturity. The human's part in this sanctification is consecration or devotement. God is the one who does the purifying, first of the intentions and then of the life lived out of these intentions."[12]

10. Dunn 1998, 625-68.
11. Dunn 1998, 635-48.
12. Leclerc 2010, 205.

Paul's prayer, then, is profoundly holistic. It is not simply about cultivating deeper affection but about fostering a love that is wise, holy, and fruitful. Writing from prison, Paul models the very wisdom he commends. He interprets his suffering not as failure but as participation in God's redemptive plan (Phil. 1:12-14). This is the heart of Christian discernment: seeing life through the lens of Christ's self-giving love.

In a culture that often equates love with permissiveness, Paul insists that true love must be wise. As John Wesley taught, holiness involves all inward and outward conformity to Christ, requiring both moral clarity and gracious action.[13] In African contexts, for example, where churches may need to challenge exploitative traditional practices or systemic corruption, this discerning love provides a framework for holy engagement without compromise. A young leader who confronts corruption with humility, grace, and truth embodies this kind of gospel-shaped discernment.

Paul's aim is ultimately eschatological: that believers may be ready "for the day of Christ" (Phil. 1:10). As Michael Gorman observes, such discernment is "cruciform"—shaped by the cross and rooted in God's future breaking into our present.[14] To love like Christ requires not just knowing facts about God but living in relationship with him. This love, infused with divine knowledge and discernment, is the very fruit of transformation by grace, for the glory and praise of God.

One of the most profound examples of gospel partnership and discernment I have witnessed comes from the 1991 Regional Conference of the Church of the Nazarene in Africa. At this pivotal gathering, more than two thousand Nazarenes from

13. Wesley (1872) 1984b.

14. Gorman 2015, 27.

twenty-four countries engaged in a bold and Spirit-guided conversation titled "Holiness Lifestyle in the African Context." Recognizing that holy living must be both faithful to Scripture and responsive to cultural realities, the church convened a panel of African leaders—pastors, educators, and laypersons—to address complex questions about traditional customs, ethics, and Christian witness.

The questions were not easy: Could Christians participate in ceremonies like the Reed Dance,[15] which involved immodest attire and ancestral symbolism? What about holding night vigils, tombstone unveilings, and cleansing rituals[16] after death? Were these compatible with the gospel? Were Christians free to wear traditional attire, or were they required to adopt Western norms?

The African church did not respond with simplistic decrees. Instead, they demonstrated a model of discernment deeply rooted in prayer, Scripture, and the wisdom of sanctified leaders. Responses emphasized that culture is not inherently sinful, but when sin infiltrates culture, believers are called to renounce it for the sake of Christ. As one leader stated, "We keep our unique amoral culture and the things that are good within it," but we must "do away with all sinful elements in our culture" when we come to Christ.

These leaders modeled what Paul described in Philippians 1:9-11—a love that abounds "in knowledge and depth of insight," enabling believers to discern what is excellent and to be "pure and blameless for the day of Christ" (vv. 9-10, NIV). They did not

15. A cultural festival where young women perform traditional dances before the royal family, with implications of ancestral reverence and royal courtship.

16. A traditional African ritual performed after death, often involving feasts or symbolic acts believed to protect the bereaved from ancestral spirits or misfortune.

merely apply abstract theology; they wrestled with concrete, lived realities—family expectations, communal pressures, and deeply rooted customs. With pastoral clarity and moral courage, they affirmed that holiness does not require the adoption of Western styles but does require moral integrity, spiritual wisdom, and a fearless trust in God's grace.

One response about funeral customs noted that if the motive behind a ritual was rooted in fear of the dead or ancestral veneration, then Christians should not participate. In many African communities, certain mourning practices, such as night vigils, ceremonial cleansing of the bereaved family, or extravagant unveiling ceremonies, are often driven by fear of ancestral spirits or spiritual retribution. These rituals, though deeply woven into the fabric of communal life, can unintentionally perpetuate a theology of fear, where the dead are believed to exert control over the living. In these cases, cultural customs are not merely expressions of grief or remembrance but spiritual transactions based on appeasement.

African church leaders recognized this tension and provided a redemptive response. Rather than dismissing cultural expressions of grief wholesale, they called for discernment rooted in the gospel. When motives are driven by fear, manipulation, or superstition, believers are encouraged to break with such practices—not out of cultural contempt, but out of loyalty to Christ. Christians are to embrace a new narrative: one grounded in the resurrection of Jesus, the victory over death, and the assurance of eternal life. In place of fear, the church offers prayer, love, simplicity, and community support.

This is not cultural rejection—it is cultural redemption. It is the transformation of mourning rituals into expressions of hope. For example, instead of ritual feasts to cleanse or appease the dead, believers might gather for a memorial service centered on gratitude to God and pastoral care for the grieving. The shift is profound: from fear of the dead to faith in the risen Christ, from obligation to freedom, and from manipulation to grace.

This kind of discernment is the fruit of a sanctified imagination—one that sees every cultural practice through the lens of Christ's death and resurrection. It embodies what Paul meant by being "filled with the fruit of righteousness" and prepares believers to stand "blameless for the day of Christ" (vv. 10-11, NIV). In doing so, the African church is not erasing culture but allowing the gospel to refine and renew it.

The church's collective discernment process was a vivid demonstration of gospel partnership—leaders and congregations walking together in grace, empowered by the Spirit to bear witness to Christ in every facet of life. Their courage reminds us that holy living is not about conforming to external models, but about being transformed from within and living wisely, lovingly, and faithfully in our context.

This is what it means to be a holy people—not a people without culture, but a people redeemed within culture, discerning with the mind of Christ and bearing witness to God's kingdom in every place. It is a vision of holiness that is as bold as it is beautiful.

Conclusion

We give thanks for the generations of believers who have gone before us—those who lived the gospel with courage and conviction, who prayed, gave, suffered, and persevered for the sake of Christ. Their lives remind us that holiness is not an abstract ideal but a life formed by grace, lived in faithful partnership with others, and marked by tangible witness to the gospel.

I thank God for you—for your faithful participation in God's redemptive mission. You, too, are partners in grace.

Perhaps today you feel weary, disillusioned, or uncertain. The world presses in with discouragement, compromise, or fear. But take heart: the One who began a good work in you is not finished. God is faithful. His grace is not only sufficient but also powerful, purifying, and persistent. It sustains us through suffering, strengthens us in weakness, and carries us toward completion.

The church is not called to retreat into fear or self-preservation. We are called to become the gospel for the sake of the world—to reflect God's holiness, to grow in love shaped by knowledge and moral insight, and to make decisions that flow from a life anchored in Christ and empowered by the Spirit.

So, as you continue to walk the path of faith, remember this: You do not walk alone. You are part of a Spirit-formed community—called, consecrated, and commissioned. May God's transforming grace continue to work in you and through you so that your life may bear witness to the gospel in both word and deed, until the day of Christ.

BIBLIOGRAPHY

Asamoah-Gyadu, J. Kwabena. 2013. *Contemporary Pentecostal Christianity: Interpretations from an African Context*. Oxford, UK: Regnum Books.

Barclay, John M. G. 2015. *Paul and the Gift*. Grand Rapids: Eerdmans.

Bauckham, Richard. 1998. *God Crucified: Monotheism and Christology in the New Testament*. Carlisle, UK: Paternoster.

———. 2008. *Jesus and the God of Israel*. Grand Rapids: Eerdmans.

Bediako, Kwame. 1995. *Christianity in Africa: The Renewal of a Non-Western Religion*. Edinburgh: Edinburgh University Press.

Broodryk, Johann. 2006. *Ubuntu: Life-Coping Skills from Africa*. Randburg, ZA: Knowres.

Brower, Kent E. 2005. *Holiness in the Gospels*. Kansas City: Beacon Hill Press of Kansas City.

———. 2009. *Living as God's Holy People: Holiness and Community in Paul*. The 2008 Didsbury Lectures. Milton Keynes: Authentic Media.

———. 2014. "Holiness and Community in 1 John." Pages 127-42 in *The Path of Holiness: Perspectives in Wesleyan Thought in Honor of Herbert B. McGonigle*. Edited by Joseph W. Cunningham and David Rainey. Lexington, KY: Emeth.

Collins, Kenneth J. 2007. *The Theology of John Wesley: Holy Love and the Shape of Grace*. Nashville: Abingdon.

Dunn, James D. G. 1998. *The Theology of Paul the Apostle*. Grand Rapids: Eerdmans.

Dunning, H. Ray. 1988. *Grace, Faith, and Holiness: A Wesleyan Systematic Theology*. Kansas City: Beacon Hill Press of Kansas City.

———. 1991. *A Layman's Guide to Sanctification*. Kansas City: Beacon Hill Press of Kansas City.

Fee, Gordon D. 1995. *Paul's Letter to the Philippians*. The New International Commentary on the New Testament. Grand Rapids: Eerdmans.

Flemming, Dean. 2005. *Contextualization in the New Testament: Patterns for Theology and Mission*. Downers Grove, IL: InterVarsity.

———. 2009. *Philippians: A Commentary in the Wesleyan Tradition*. New Beacon Bible Commentary. Kansas City: Beacon Hill Press of Kansas City.

———. 2013. *Recovering the Full Mission of God*. Downers Grove, IL: IVP Academic.

Foster, Richard J. 1985. *Money, Sex and Power: The Challenge of the Disciplined Life*. San Francisco: Harper and Row.

Garland, David E. 1999. *2 Corinthians*. The New American Commentary 29. Nashville: B. and H.

Gaventa, Beverly Roberts. 2003. *The Acts of the Apostles*. Abingdon New Testament Commentaries. Nashville: Abingdon.

Gorman, Michael J. 2001. *Cruciformity: Paul's Narrative Spirituality of the Cross*. Grand Rapids: Eerdmans.

———. 2015. *Becoming the Gospel: Paul, Participation, and Mission*. Grand Rapids: Eerdmans.

Green, Joel B. 1997. *The Gospel of Luke*. The New International Commentary on the New Testament. Grand Rapids: Eerdmans.

———. 2015. *Conversion in Luke-Acts: Divine Action, Human Cognition, and the People of God*. Grand Rapids: Baker Academic.

Grenz, Stanley J. 2001. *The Social God and the Relational Self: A Trinitarian Theology of the* Imago Dei. Louisville, KY: Westminster John Knox Press.

Hays, Richard B. 1996. *The Moral Vision of the New Testament: A Contemporary Introduction to New Testament Ethics*. New York: HarperOne.

Isichei, Elizabeth. 1995. *A History of Christianity in Africa: From Antiquity to the Present*. Grand Rapids: Eerdmans.

Jobes, Karen H. 2005. *1 Peter*. Baker Exegetical Commentary on the New Testament. Grand Rapids: Baker Academic.

Johnson, E. Elizabeth. 2020. *Ecclesiology in the New Testament*. Nashville: Abingdon.

Johnson, Luke Timothy. 1992. *The Acts of the Apostles*. Sacra Pagina 5. Collegeville, MN: Liturgical Press.

Joseph, Abson Prédestin. 2012. *A Narratological Reading of 1 Peter*. Library of New Testament Studies 440. New York: T. and T. Clark.

Katongole, Emmanuel. 2011. *The Sacrifice of Africa: A Political Theology for Africa*. Grand Rapids: Eerdmans.

Khoza, Reuel J. 2006. *Let Africa Lead: African Transformational Leadership for 21st Century Business*. Johannesburg, ZA: Vezubuntu.

Kim, Kyoung-Jin. 1998. *Stewardship and Almsgiving in Luke's Theology.* Journal for the Study of the New Testament Supplement Series 155. Sheffield, UK: Sheffield Academic Press.

Kinlaw, Dennis. 1985. *Preaching in the Spirit.* Wilmore, KY: Francis Asbury.

———. 2005. *Let's Start with Jesus: A New Way of Doing Theology.* Grand Rapids: Zondervan.

Kraybill, Donald B., and Dennis M. Sweetland. 1983. "Possessions in Luke-Acts: A Sociological Perspective," *Perspectives in Religious Studies* 10, no. 3 (Fall): 215-39.

Kunhiyop, Samuel Waje. 2008. *African Christian Ethics.* Grand Rapids: Zondervan.

Ladd, George E. 1993. *A Theology of the New Testament.* Rev. ed. Grand Rapids: Eerdmans.

Leclerc, Diane. 2010. *Discovering Christian Holiness: The Heart of Wesleyan-Holiness Theology.* Kansas City: Beacon Hill Press of Kansas City.

Leclerc, Diane, and Mark A. Maddix. 2011. *Spiritual Formation: A Wesleyan Paradigm.* Kansas City: Beacon Hill Press of Kansas City.

Leclerc, Diane, and Brent Peterson. 2022. *The Back Side of the Cross: An Atonement Theology for the Abused and Abandoned.* Eugene, OR: Cascade Books.

Maddox, Randy L. 1994. *Responsible Grace: John Wesley's Practical Theology.* Nashville: Kingswood Books.

Mana, Kä. 2002. *Christians and the Challenge of Political Life in Africa Today.* Nairobi, KE: Paulines Publications Africa.

Mbiti, John S. 1990. *African Religions and Philosophy.* 2nd ed. Oxford, UK: Heinemann.

Mtukwa, Gift. 2014. "Ancestral Cult and the Church in Africa." *Africa Journal of Wesleyan Theology* 1, no. 1 (March): 7-24.

———. 2023. "Past, Present, and Future: Paul's View of Salvation in the Thessalonian Correspondence." Pages 111-32 in *Salvation in African Christianity.* Edited by Rodney L. Reed and David K. Ngaruiya. Carlisle, UK: Langham Global Library.

Nave, Guy D., Jr. 2002. *The Role and Function of Repentance in Luke-Acts.* Atlanta: Society of Biblical Literature.

Noble, T. A. 2013. *Holy Trinity: Holy People: The Theology of Christian Perfecting.* The 2012 Didsbury Lectures. Eugene, OR: Cascade Books.

———. 2025a. "Holiness and the Holy Trinity." Keynote address presented at Tyndale Wesley Studies Symposium, Tyndale Seminary, Toronto, April 29, 2025. https://www2.tyndale.ca/sites/default/files/2025-04/Noble_Keynote_Address_Wesley_Sympoisum_2025_0.pdf.

———. 2025b. *Jesus Christ.* Kansas City: Foundry.

Nouwen, Henri J. M. 1992. *Life of the Beloved: Spiritual Living in a Secular World.* New York: Crossroad.

O'Brien, P. T. 1991. *The Epistle to the Philippians: A Commentary on the Greek Text.* The New International Greek Testament Commentary. Grand Rapids: Eerdmans.

Oden, Thomas C. 1994. *John Wesley's Scriptural Christianity: A Plain Exposition of His Teaching on Christian Doctrine.* Grand Rapids: Zondervan.

Ogden, Greg. 2003. *Transforming Discipleship: Making Disciples a Few at a Time.* Downers Grove, IL: InterVarsity Press.

Ok, Janette H. 2021. *Constructing Ethnic Identity in 1 Peter: Who You Are No Longer.* Library of New Testament Studies 645. London: Bloomsbury Academic.

Phillips, Thomas E. 2001. *Reading Issues of Wealth and Poverty in Luke-Acts.* Lewiston, NY: Edwin Mellen.

Scheffler, Eben H. 1990. "The Socio-Ethics of the Lucan Baptist." *Neotestamentica* 24 (1): 21-36.

Schenone, Osvaldo, and Samuel Gregg. 2003. *A Theory of Corruption: The Theology and Economics of Sin.* Christian Social Thought Series 7. Grand Rapids: Action Institute.

Shoemaker, Mel. 1992. "Good News to the Poor in Luke's Gospel." *Wesleyan Theological Journal* 27, nos. 1-2 (Spring-Fall): 181-205.

Shoemaker, Stephen J. 2012. *The Death of a Prophet: The End of Muhammad's Life and the Beginnings of Islam.* Philadelphia: University of Pennsylvania Press.

Smalley, Stephen S. 1991. *1, 2, 3 John.* Word Biblical Commentary. Waco, TX: Word.

Taylor, Charles. 2007. *A Secular Age.* Cambridge, MA: Harvard University Press.

Tiénou, Tite. 1990. *The Theological Task of the Church in Africa.* Achimota, GH: Africa Christian.

———. 2004. "Integrity of Mission in Light of the Gospel in Africa: A Perspective from an African in Diaspora." Paper presented at the Eleventh International Conference of the International Association of Mission Studies, Port Dickson, Malaysia, August.

———. 2006. "Christian Theology in an Era of World Christianity." Pages 37-51 in *Globalizing Theology: Belief and Practice in an Era of World Christianity*. Edited by Craig Ott and Harold A. Netland. Grand Rapids: Baker Academic.

Tutu, Desmond. 1995. *An African Prayer Book*. New York: Doubleday.

———. 1999. *No Future without Forgiveness*. New York: Doubleday.

Tyerman, Luke. 1872. *The Life and Times of the Rev. John Wesley, M.A., Founder of the Methodists*. Vol. 3. New York: Harper and Brothers.

Wall, Robert W. 2000. "Reading the Bible from within Our Traditions: The 'Rule of Faith' in Theological Hermeneutics." In *Between Two Horizons: Spanning New Testament Studies and Systematic Theology*. Edited by Joel B. Green and Max Turner. Grand Rapids: Eerdmans.

Walls, Andrew F. 1976. "Towards Understanding Africa's Place in Christian History." Pages 180-89 in *Religion in a Pluralistic Society: Essays Presented to Professor C. G. Baëta*. Edited by J. S. Pobee. Leiden, NL: Brill.

———. 1996. *The Missionary Movement in Christian History: Studies in the Transmission of Faith*. Maryknoll, NY: Orbis Books.

Warrington, Keith. 2009. *The Message of the Holy Spirit*. Downers Grove, IL: InterVarsity.

Wenk, Matthias. 2000. *Community-Forming Power: The Socio-Ethical Role of the Spirit in Luke-Acts*. Journal of Pentecostal Theology 19. Sheffield: Sheffield Academic.

Wesley, John. (1872) 1984a. *The Character of a Methodist*. Pages 340-47 of vol. 8 in *The Works of John Wesley*. 3rd ed. Edited by Thomas Jackson. London: Wesleyan Methodist Book Room. Reprint, Peabody, MA: Hendrickson.

———. (1872) 1984b. "The Circumcision of the Heart." Pages 202-12 of vol. 5 in *The Works of John Wesley*. 3rd ed. Edited by Thomas Jackson. London: Wesleyan Methodist Book Room. Reprint, Peabody, MA: Hendrickson.

———. (1872) 1984c. Preface to *Hymns and Sacred Poems*. Pages 319-22 of vol. 14 in *The Works of John Wesley*. 3rd ed. Edited by Thomas Jackson. London: Wesleyan Methodist Book Room. Reprint, Peabody, MA: Hendrickson.

———. (1872) 1984d. "Thoughts upon Methodism." Pages 258-61 of vol. 13 in *The Works of John Wesley*. 3rd ed. Edited by Thomas Jackson. London: Wesleyan Methodist Book Room. Reprint, Peabody, MA: Hendrickson.

———. 1991a. "The Image of God." Pages 14-21 in *John Wesley's Sermons: An Anthology*. Edited by Albert C. Outler and Richard P. Heitzenrater. Nashville: Abingdon.

———. 1991b. "The New Birth." Pages 336-45 in *John Wesley's Sermons: An Anthology*. Edited by Albert C. Outler and Richard P. Heitzenrater. Nashville: Abingdon.

———. 1991c. "The Scripture Way of Salvation." Pages 372-80 in *John Wesley's Sermons: An Anthology*. Edited by Albert C. Outler and Richard P. Heitzenrater. Nashville: Abingdon.

———. 1991d. "The Use of Money." Pages 348-57 in *John Wesley's Sermons: An Anthology*. Edited by Albert C. Outler and Richard P. Heitzenrater. Nashville: Abingdon.

Wi, MiJa. 2019a. *The Path to Salvation in Luke: What Must We Do?* Library of New Testament Studies 621. London: T. and T. Clark.

———. 2019b. "You Shall Receive Power to Cross the Boundaries (Acts 1:8): The Holy Spirit as the Boundary Crosser and the Boundary Marker." *Didache: Faithful Teaching* 19, no. 1 (Spring 2019/Winter 2020): https://didache.nazarene.org/index.php/filedownload/didache-volumes/vol-19/1268-didache-v19n1-2-09-holy-spirit-boundary-crossing-wi/file.

Witherington, Ben, III. 1995. *Conflict and Community in Corinth: A Socio-Rhetorical Commentary on 1 and 2 Corinthians*. Grand Rapids: Eerdmans.

Wright, Christopher J. H. 2006. *The Mission of God: Unlocking the Bible's Grand Narrative*. Downers Grove, IL: IVP Academic.

Wright, N. T. 2010. *After You Believe: Why Christian Character Matters*. New York: HarperOne.

———. 2011. "Whence and Whither Pauline Studies in the Life of the Church?" Pages 262-81 in *Jesus, Paul and the People of God: A Theological Dialogue with N. T. Wright*. Edited by Nicholas Perrin and Richard B. Hays. Downers Grove, IL: InterVarsity.

———. 2013. *Paul and the Faithfulness of God*. Minneapolis: Fortress.

———. 2014. *What Saint Paul Really Said: Was Paul of Tarsus the Real Founder of Christianity?* Grand Rapids: Eerdmans.

Yoder, John Howard. 1994. *The Politics of Jesus*. 2nd ed. Grand Rapids: Eerdmans.

www.ingramcontent.com/pod-product-compliance
Lightning Source LLC
LaVergne TN
LVHW051418080426
835508LV00022B/3141

9780834144019